AMOR FATI

ATROPOS PRESS
new york • dresden

AMOR FATI

Eternal Procession in Emerson and Nietzsche

CAROLINE S. KELLEY

ATROPOS

new york | dresden

ATROPOS PRESS
NEW YORK | DRESDEN

GENERAL EDITOR:
WOLFGANG SCHIRMACHER

EXECUTIVE EDITOR:
ANDREW SPANO

EDITORIAL BOARD:
GIORGIO AGAMBEN
PIERRE ALFERI
HUBERTUS VON AMELUNXEN
ALAIN BADIOU
JUDITH BALSO
JUDITH BUTLER
DIANE DAVIS
MARTIN HIELSCHER
GEERT LOVINK
LARRY RICKELS
AVITAL RONELL
MICHAEL SCHMIDT
FRIEDRICH ULFERS
VICTOR VITANZA
SIEGFRIED ZIELINSKI
SLAVOJ ŽIŽEK

THINK MEDIA SERIES IS SUPPORTED BY THE EUROPEAN
GRADUATE SCHOOL

ATROPOS PRESS
151 FIRST AVENUE # 14, NEW YORK, N.Y. 10003
MOCKRITZER STR. 6, D-01219, DRESDEN, GERMANY

BOOK INTERIOR DESIGN BY: ANDJELA

TABLE OF CONTENTS

Part III. ARIADNE

Part IV. CIRCLES

Part V. WOMAN

ABBREVIATIONS

Emerson's Works

W= Ralph Waldo Emerson, *The Complete Works of Ralph Waldo Emerson,* edited by Edward Waldo Emerson and Waldo Emerson Forbes, 12 volumes, 1909, The Digital Library Text Collection at The University of Michigan. Followed by volume number: page number.

JMN= Ralph Waldo Emerson, *The Journals and Miscellaneous Notebooks of Ralph Waldo Emerson,* edited by William H. Gilman, Ralph H. Orth et al., 16 volumes, 1960-82, Cambridge, Mass.: Harvard University Press. Followed by volume number: page number.

L = Ralph Waldo Emerson, *The Letters of Ralph Waldo Emerson*, edited by Ralph L. Rusk and Eleanor M. Tilton, 10 volumes, 1939 and 1990-5, New York: Columbia University Press. Followed by volume number: page number.

Nietzsche's Works

KSA= *Kritische Studienausgabe,* compiled under the general editorship of Giorgio Colli and Mazzino Montinari and based on the complete edition of the *Kritische Gesamtausgabe* (KGW)(Berlin and New York: Walter de Gruyter, 1967ff). Volume number followed by the relevant fragment number and any relevant aphorism.

BGE = *Jenseits von Gut und Böse*; translated as *Beyond Good and Evil.* Followed by aphorism number.

BT = *Die Geburt der Tragödie*; translated as *The Birth of Tragedy.* Followed by aphorism number.

GM = *Zur Genealogie der Moral*; frequently translated as *On the Genealogy of Morals or On the Genealogy of Morality.* Followed by aphorism number.

GS = *Die fröhliche Wissenschaft*; frequently translated as *The Gay Science* or *The Joyful Wisdom*. Followed by aphorism number.

HH = *Menschliches, Allzumenschliches*; translated as *Human, All Too Human*. Followed by aphorism number.

TI = *Götzen-Dämmerung*; translated as *Twilight of The Idols*; references to this work also include an abbreviated section name followed by aphorism number.

Z = *Also sprach Zarathustra* (part IV originally published privately); translated as *Thus Spoke Zarathustra*; references to this work also include an abbreviated section name followed by aphorism number.

EH = *Ecce Homo*; references to this work also include an abbreviated section name followed by aphorism number.

Fragments of Heraclitus

B= *Fragment from Heraclitus*, and T.M. Robinson. 1991. *Heraclitus: fragments: a text and translation with a commentary.* Toronto: University of Toronto Press. Followed by fragment number, e.g. B1.

INTRODUCTION

Friedrich Nietzsche read and reread Ralph Waldo Emerson's first series of essays throughout his life, most diligently while composing *The Gay Science*, *Thus Spake Zarathustra* and *Beyond Good and Evil*, underlining phrases and marking avid notes in his copy of the book. It has long been known that he was influenced by his reading of Emerson's *Versuche*, yet while prominent scholars have found instances where Nietzsche's phrasing has been lifted directly from Emerson's works, they have been reluctant to Identify a meaningful legacy, preferring to imagine a vague, if avuncular, relation between them[1]. The impact of Emerson on Nietzsche's philosophy and the corresponding impact of Nietzsche on Emerson's philosophy has been diminished or otherwise damned by this faint association.

The cultural reputations of these iconic writers remain vastly different. At large, Emerson is taken to be the natural heir of Protestant philosophy whose thinking was metaphysical and Nietzsche is esteemed for his critical prowess at the expense of his spiritual teachings. There is a resistance to reading Emerson as a critic of Christian morality as a result of the genteel tradition in which he has been placed, just as there is a resistance to reading Nietzsche as defending benevolence because of the war he wages on morality. The father of the ambiguous philosophy of Transcendentalism, whose essays American high school students read reluctantly, plays the good guy, while the sire of the equally ambiguous philosophy of eternal return, whose one work of fiction was studied by Nazi soldiers, plays the bad guy. Both Emerson and Nietzsche are condemned to a kind of infamy that discredits the reach of their thought.

The academic reputations of their work are also starkly different. Nietzsche is perceived as a genius whose thinking ran parallel to the development of quantum mechanics, while Emerson is taken as an inspirational writer whose kind-hearted exhortations conveyed

---

1   "Most scholars exaggerate the kinship of these men." Walter Arnold Kaufmann, introduction to Nietzsche, Friedrich, *The Gay Science with A Prelude in Rhymes and An Appendix of Songs*, trans. Walter Kaufmann (New York: Random House,1974), 3.

his rather imaginative religious convictions. Nietzsche is revered as the moody master of continental philosophy while Emerson is dismissed as a quaint spiritualist. That they were both radical thinkers is undisputed, but their affiliation seems to embarrass scholars on both sides of the Emerson-Nietzsche connection as if it might deny a guilty pleasure in reading Emerson for his sentimentality and Nietzsche for his contempt.

In their extremes, Nietzsche comes off as caustic and Emerson as frivolous. But they are not completely unlike in their styles: both are circuitous, allusionary, playful, forceful and fragmentary. They address their readers directly. Neither writes like a conventional philosopher: their prose is heated with emotion, and punctual in its rhythm. There is no drive to argument, no point to prove, rather, an operatic intellect that cuts through dimensions of thought. Emerson exhales metaphors that arise like froth in his flowing prose; he makes light of his nouns, but the careful, simple half-phrases sink like lead in their depths. Nietzsche writes like an early modernist. His aphorisms are numbered; their order has a Pythagorean consistency. Both are mythical minded. One is concise in his criticism, the other extravagant in his eulogy. While Emerson spins like a dervish in the here and now, Nietzsche blasts from his mountaintop by the fire of his impulsive wit, to bring, as Kaufmann wrote, philosophy down to earth.[2]

Questions of style color the distinctions between the two writers, but their aesthetics do not express dissimilar orientations. Though the tragic worldview is attributed as the position that made Nietzsche so prickly, Emerson's circumstances were no less tragic. Both wrote on the eve of catastrophic war, were radical intellectuals and romantic spirits raised in the Protestant tradition by minister-fathers who died when they were young. Both were antinomian in a Kantian sense (they embraced contradiction) and in a religious sense (they were apostates). They believed in the importance of a kind of aesthetic knowledge that operates as an impulse to play. Indeed, they can be said to be saying the same thing in different ways regarding the question of how to live in a complex that they both call fate.

Fatalism for Emerson and Nietzsche means something fairly

---

2   Walter Kaufmann, *Nietzsche, Philosopher, Psychologist, Antichrist* (Princeton: Princeton University Press, 2018), 8.

precise. Acceptance of one's end institutes an integrity that sustains the illusion of subjectivity grounded in the love that is inherent in nature, appropriated for the purpose of freedom, progress, and benefit. Some responsibility is assumed for the "I" that invigorates change, propelling the course of things auspiciously. This responsibility entails an education in how to proceed cheerfully in the world without paralyzing a critical response to it.

Their practice of skepticism extended to the term itself. Both writers identified different kinds of fatalism. Emerson's Turkish fatalist fervently seeks an end to suffering, falling on his sword, while Nietzsche's Russian fatalist embraces his suffering if only to survive his infirmity. But the kind of refined fatalism that Emerson calls "the Beautiful Necessity" and Nietzsche calls *amor fati* is ethics embodied, an attempt to engage what is actually good.

Actual good is aligned with circumstance and can change. For Emerson, it is physically felt. Human beings are endowed with a "moral sentiment" that directs them: one knows intrinsically what is right and what is wrong if one is receptive to "intelligence and good will at the heart of things" (W 12:1). For Nietzsche, good deeds emerge from an "education of the will" (WP 4:2), a matter of learning to see rather than merely to react. Learning to see engages affective insight, a sort of Heraclitan "contuition" that involves the cultivation of the impulses.

Amor fati can be understood as a willingness to perform as a part of the whole, which required for Nietzsche "freedom from resentment" (EH "Wise" 6). Emerson's "Beautiful Necessity" did not frame it so negatively: freedom is not the relinquishment of bad feelings but a dedication to courage that enables one to proceed from a spirit of benevolence according to a morality reformed from weary Christian valuations. While Nietzsche's negativity was acutely honest, Emerson's focus on the positive seemed to deny suffering altogether. The "Happiness Pill" that Kenneth Burke identified as the substance of Emersonian thought, and conditionally recommended, is medicine taken to palliate the damaging effects of a morality structured around a capitalistic system of values.[3] This kind of positivity acts like Theodor

---

3   Kenneth Burke, "I, Eye, Ay: Emerson's Early Essay on 'Nature': Thoughts on the Machinery of Transcendence," *The Sewanee Review* 74, no. 4 (1966): 875-895.

Adorno's "prescribed happiness,"[4] a false enthusiasm that bolsters the domination of false values that confuse what is good with what makes money. But Emersonian "necessity" was neither a lusty materialism nor a coarse Darwinism, rather it was a graceful consent to both the demise and re-creation of the self. He did not deny suffering but qualified it in the light of felicity.

Emerson's public optimism was persistent despite the pangs of his "Experience." He was a fabulous yes-sayer: the essay ends with these lines: "there is victory yet for all justice; and the true romance which the world exists to realize will be the transformation of genius into practical power" (p. 86). It is this process of becoming rather than its product that interested Emerson. In "Experience," he distanced himself from the fruits of his work, focusing on the dynamics of "vigor" (p. 73) in the realm of conscience. His ethics effect ongoing conversion. Contrary to classic American scholarship, he should not be classified as a pragmatist. Pragmatism focuses on the act, while Emerson's more romantic philosophy concerns itself with the "dignity of any deed" (p. 73). Discernment is involved.

Emerson's radical ideas were developed in *Nature*, his first published work, which elaborates on the plasticity of language as the material of the natural world. In the progression of his lecturing career, nature shifted course. First it was thoroughly mediate, Emerson's plastic vision, then it became powerful in its own right as "philosophy and theology embodied," (W 4:49) overwhelming the powers of human code. He emerges after the four books of *Nature* as a kind of Prospero, the survivor of a corrupt regime who governs the spirits of nature then cedes control. As Prospero released Ariel from the cloven pine, Emersonian insight liberated nature from the church. His final appeal in "Experience," "Never mind the ridicule, never mind the defeat: up again, old heart" (p. 86) echoes Prospero's last line, "Let your indulgence set me free," to relinquish his fate enthusiastically to the hands of others.

Nietzsche's indulgence in Emerson's affirmation of life came across in his first published declaration of *amor fati* in *Die Fröhliche Wissenschaft*, or *The Gay Science*:

---

4   Theodor Adorno, *Minima Moralia: Reflections from A Damaged Life*, trans. E.F.N. Jephcott (London: Verso Books,1974), 38.

I want to learn more and more to see as beautiful what is necessary in things:— then I shall be one of those who make things beautiful. *Amor fati*: let that be my love from henceforth! I do not want to wage war (Krieg) against what is ugly. I do not want to accuse, I do not even want to accuse those who accuse. Looking away shall be my only negation! And all in all and on the whole: some day I wish to be only a Yes-sayer! (276)

The book was formulated as a kind of seduction, modeled after *la gaya scienza* of the Troubadours; the "Joyous science," a phrase that occurs in Emerson's lecture "Prospects" and essay "The Scholar," is an alternate translation of the title. Though it is unclear whether Nietzsche derived the term from Emerson, the "Joyous science" is recommended by both writers as a kind of self-seduction that is at once enthusiastic and skeptical.

In Nietzsche's revision of *The Gay Science*, he was seduced by his re-reading of Emerson towards an acceptance of the terms of his seduction, i.e., *die fröhliche wissenschaft* as the enlightened search for happiness, framed as the more temperamental cheerfulness. His original ironic stance towards the science of happiness became an earnest investigation whose denial of happiness performed its own recovery by way of the humorous pathos of distance. The intense disappointment described in the Januarius section is the abyss from which *amor fati* delivered him. His New Year's cheer was not a Stoic reconciliation, but a romantic inclination humored by re-conceptions of the *gaya scienza* as a mitigation of the grotesque, a redemption of the body and celebration of an actuality that denies everything except a conditional benevolence at the heart of things. His reception of Emersonian fatalism was tentative, but powerful, and when elaborated, became the crux of his philosophy.

The seven recorded statements of *amor fati*, from its formation in the *Nachlass* to its published versions in *The Gay Science*, *Ecce Homo*, "Nietzsche contra Wagner" and *Will to Power*, characterize the phrase as an aesthetics of aversion, a "moral" affirmation" (KSA 9:13 [20]), a metaphysical love of wisdom, and an ideation of necessity that proposes eternal return. The ultimate instruction of *amor fati* proposes that every experience and pain is necessary for one to become what one is:

> My formula for greatness in a human being is *amor fati*: that one wants nothing to be different, not forward, not backward, not in all eternity. Not merely bear what is necessary, still less conceal it—all idealism is mendaciousness in the face of what is necessary—but love it (EH "Books" 10).

This includes the pricks of doubt that the lover feels about the meaning of life. In spite of the suffering, "even the love of life is still possible—only, one loves differently ... It is the love for a woman who raises doubts in us" (GS Preface). This blessed state of uncertainty encourages the cultivation of faith in oneself even as it demands suspicion.

The self-blessing of *amor fati* seeks to answer the question of how to live by enacting the performance of becoming, cheerfully. The intellectual inquiry into happiness in the hands of Emerson and Nietzsche was complicated by the absence of a traditional God and an embrace of ancient philosophy, particularly newly translated texts by Heraclitus who supplied the aphorism that engaged them: "character is destiny" (B121). Transposed by the synonymous meanings of "destiny" and "fate," *amor fati* becomes "love of character" or love of one's possibilities.

For Emerson, character is expressed energetically as a "magnetism" (W 3:91) that is aligned more to nature than to society, an innate sensibility that encourages resistance. Character is grounded in temperament, which represents "the chain of physical necessity" (W 2:55) that can nonetheless be altered: it interacts with the Oversoul to engender "Being," a fluctuating force that never arrives as an absolute state. Like "a bird which alights nowhere, but hops perpetually from bough to bough" (p. 58), the Oversoul is present but not accounted for.

For Nietzsche, character is physical, and power moves more like a raptor than Emerson's sprightly bird. Nietzschean character is Dionysian, and its power is contained in a will that suffers the dynamics of change in a nature that operates as passion. In contrast with the romantic pessimist, the Dionysian pessimist eschews vengeance in order to make radical change. Critical thinking and instinct inform a revaluation of values that attempts to vitalize the spirit. The Dionysian spirit, "pregnant with the future" (GS 370) is the condition in which will to power and its lack—the contradiction that composes *amor fati*—produce an interplay with possibility, becoming the human position of creation.

A new kind of character emerged from Nietzsche's reading of Emerson that encourages submission to the complexities of nature. As Nietzsche wrote on the back of his copy of Emerson's *Versuche*:

> Not to see the new greatness above oneself, not to see it outside oneself, rather to make of it a new function of one's self. We are the ocean into which all great rivers must flow. How dangerous it is when our faith in our own universality fails! A plurality of faiths are required" (KSA 9:13[19]).

A novel self-conception is required to accommodate "the ocean" of "our own universality" that is contained in the Dionysian spirit. *Amor fati* acted as Nietzsche's surrender of his own acuity to circumstances that determine. He returned to his martial language to utter the compact phrase. With the mastery of the general—avoiding all tricks of conscience— he directed a yes to every proposition, negation, mood and inclination to beget a self beyond itself. Simultaneously recognizing the scalar value of his personal agonies, and the vector of existence by acknowledging necessity, Nietzsche understood the limits of his will. In effect, the decree of *amor fati* declares: I am that, an ambiguous possibility, which, in Vedic philosophy, is a mantra identifying its speaker with the infinite other.

The female other, however, presented a problem for Nietzsche. As the Sphinx, she represents deception. As the *vita femina*, she is nebulous, shifty, but once glimpsed, brilliant. Otherwise, again in Latin, *mulieres taceat*. Nietzsche's misogyny is well known. Whether it is justified by the domestic domineering of his mother and older sister, or his rejected hand in marriage by Lou Von Salomé, it persistently manifests in his works as a sacred devotion. Nietzsche's emphatic derision of women reveals a passion that informs *amor fati* as a sense of resistance that assails against and then relinquishes itself to life, love, truth, and woman. The passivity associated with *amor fati*, the yes-saying and accommodation, was an abrupt and coded assent to the feminine that came to him through Emerson.

Emerson acted as Nietzsche's Ariadne—his Yes—leading him through the labyrinth that looked like an abyss after the death of God. Emerson's Yes performed as a beneficial skepsis that took the magnanimous Why not? as its mood. He redeemed the illusion of "Being" that Nietzsche connected with women. Ariadne as a version of the eternal feminine is always lifting us upwards, but in Nietzsche's hermeneutics, she acts as a reversal of gravity, bringing one back to nature. This is also a reversal of gravitas: cheerfulness is required, an auspicious disposition towards all of the sufferings of life.

Cheerfulness is excellent, but "nothing succeeds unless prankishness plays a part" (HATH Preface). The pranks that Nietzsche played on his readers involve his excavation of women and sneaky deification of Emerson. Nietzsche's misogyny can be understood as deliberate provocation, a kind of prank intended as education by poison. The prank of his "genius of the heart," the man-god whose identity he tempts his readers to guess in both *Beyond Good and Evil* and *Ecce Homo*, encodes Emerson, who in *Twilight of The Idols* is already immortal: he doesn't know how young he is or how old he will be. The "gracious and clever cheerfulness, which discourages all seriousness" (13) that Nietzsche attributes to Emerson in *Twilight* echoes the "halcyon and frivolous makeup" (1038) of his dancing god, introduced in *Will to Power* just before his last exclamation of *amor fati*. All three of these figures—the "genius of the heart", the dancing god, and Emerson— are understood as the same character, indicating that Nietzsche's formulation of *amor fati*, mitigated through his orientation to the female, was profoundly influenced by Emerson.

To say Nietzschean hermeneutics are encrypted in woman is nothing new. Jacques Derrida has already connected Nietzsche's style with woman in his *Eperons, Le Style de Nietzsche*, in which he understood, as the title suggests, that Nietzsche's style was a provocation meant, "as a means of protection against the terrifying blinding mortal threat (of that) which presents itself, which obstinately thrusts itself into view".[5] Among Derrida's many references, one of the most striking is his situation of the woman of Nietzsche's text: "All of Nietzsche's investigations, and in particular, those which concern woman, are coiled in the labyrinth of an ear".[6] But both the ear and the labyrinth invoke the Ariadne of Nietzsche's poem "Ariadne's Lament" and not the Ariadne

---

5   Jacques Derrida, *Spurs Nietzsche's Styles/Eperons Les Styles de Nietzsche* (Chicago and London: The University of Chicago Press, 1978), 39.

6   Ibid., 43.

of *Ecce Homo*, the version of her who is opened in the sunlight. The obvious is in question.

This book presents an empirical study of Nietzsche's debt to Emerson that claims a kind of phallologocentrism as a metaphysics of presence. Emerson is clearly present in Nietzsche's works, especially in those references that seem, once illuminated, rather overt. The evidence of context around Nietzsche's emphatic marginalia reveals a distinct legacy that has been obscured by encultured sensibility. Stanley Cavell remarked on the general reluctance to acknowledge a connection between the two writers:

> But no matter how often this connection of Nietzsche to Emerson is stated, no matter how obvious to anyone who cares to verify it, it stays incredible, it is always in a forgotten state. This interests me almost as much as the connection itself does, since the incredibility must be grounded in a fixed conviction that Emerson is not a philosopher, that he cannot be up to the pitch of reason in European philosophy. The conviction is variously useful to American as well as European philosophers as well as to literary theorists. When one mind finds itself and loses itself in another, time and place seem to fall away— not as if history is transcended but as if it has not begun.[7]

If Cavell is right, that their connection remains "incredible" as we read, then we are deluding ourselves, we who know the connection closely. Perhaps that is the point. We read them for an aesthetic response, for emotional corroboration. We find an affirmation of ourselves in the text as an unanswered question, and turn away from the question, finding ourselves in the mood of the poet.

---

7   Stanley Cavell, "Aversive Thinking" in *Emerson's Transcendental Etudes*, (Stanford: Stanford University Press, 2003), 148.

THE ROOTS OF AMOR FATI

In his rich book, *Nietzsche & Emerson, An Elective Affinity*, George Stack noted that no scholar has closely examined the Nietzsche-Emerson connection.[8] This study aims to do exactly this. An analysis of Nietzsche's marginalia from his copy of the *Versuche* reveals a code between them that is more complex than has been understood. Nietzsche's philosophy becomes a development of Emerson's, a development that resists development as it proclaims a new way of being, grounded in Emersonian thought. This book is organized by the metaphors of the Sphinx, the "genius of the heart," Ariadne, and Circles not merely for poetic import, but because they are the instruments by which Emerson entered most convincingly into Nietzsche's logic. The following is a summary of the hermeneutics regarding *amor fati*.

The Sphinx

For Nietzsche and Emerson, the Sphinx symbolizes the problem of being and becoming. If everything is always becoming, as both writers emphasize, there is no changeless entity in a world where there is constant growth: Plato's idealism is overcome by Heraclitan flux. But in "Experience," Emerson identified "that which changes not," an issue of the "ineffable cause" (p. 72) that language cannot quite possess, nor mankind appropriate. This protean essence is not even an action, but a "vast flowing vigor," (p. 73) a mythological Euphrates whose fecundity begets adulation. Emerson called this power "Being;" Nietzsche called it will to power. They mean the same thing.

In Friedrich Ulfers' and Mark Cohen's definitive essay, "*Amor fati*, The Embracing of An Undecided Fate," they interpret *amor fati* by way of will to power, defined as substance rather than potential. Because the will to power is not contained in an individual, there is

---

8   George Stack, *Nietzsche & Emerson: An Elective Affinity* (Athens: Ohio University Press. 1992): 2.

no free will, no freedom, only the "integration of integral opposites"[9]. This coherence presents an Apollonian construct, the appearance of unity requisite for any sort of interpretation. We need it to think. Ulfers and Cohen define *amor fati* as simply "the acceptance of necessity," or, the acceptance of fate as the representation of will to power, i.e., fate as a complex substance.[10] In effect, we need the idea of fate as the illusion of unity in order to reckon with variable meanings.

The position of illusory being, the point from which one is able to interpret, requires the illusion of subjectivity. Ulfers and Cohen emphasize that this is not to be understood as a *principium individuationis*. Nietzsche rejected the idea of the individual, placing subjectivity in the body. In a note on the back of his copy of Emerson's *Versuche*, he wrote *"charakter = organismus"*.[11] This sense of subjectivity, understood in the context as akin to character, is located in the organism described in *Will to Power* as "a kind of aristocracy of 'cells' in which dominion resides" (490). The mode of subjectivity is understood as a physiological process in which "we gain the correct idea of the nature of our subject-unity, namely as regents at the head of a communality (not as 'souls' or 'life forces')" (490). Nietzsche's physical conceit develops towards an understanding of the body as multiplicity, wherein regency is a collaborative force whose primary power is the ability to command. Command is the basic mode of all living things; hierarchy is thus one of the "conditions that make possible the whole and its parts" (492). The condition for leadership is described as a broad vision, an ignorance of the activities of the parts of the whole. This generalizing vision, which conjures goals, ideals, and illusions, is stipulated as a necessary condition of subjectivity.

Emersonian "Being" is organized in a hierarchy that nature interpenetrates through whim. *Whim* is a difficult proposition;

---

9   Mark Daniel Cohen and Friedrich Ulfers, "Nietzsche's *Amor Fati*: The Embracing of An Undecided Fate," *Poiesis: A Journal of Art and Communication 9*, no. 7. (2007): 7.

10   Ibid.

11   Nietzsche Herbst 1881 13 = Emerson-Exemplar. [Ralph Waldo Emerson, *Versuche* (Essays), aus dem Englischen von G. Fabricius. Hannover: Carl Meyer, 1858. Hereafter abbreviated as KSA 9:13 [note number], e.g., KSA 9:13 [18].

Emerson himself was not satisfied with the term.[12]   His contemporary, Edgar Allan Poe, mocked it in the story, "The Imp of The Perverse,"[13] but Poe's degenerate narrators—most were addicted to narcotics or alcohol—lacked the moral intelligence that the ethical practice of whim requires. In his journal, Emerson defined *whim* as a kind of refined fatalism "to be executed by a clever person who knows how to allow the living instinct" (8:33). Whim is incorporated within a "moral sentiment": the power of virtue itself instructs the idealizing vision.

This idea is issued in "Circles" and cited by Nietzsche in "Schopenhauer as Educator" as a way of life "by abandonment," in which "'a man...never rises so high as when he knows not whither he is going'" (p. 322). The conception of fate that Nietzsche received combines an aesthetic appropriation of free will with an affirmation of "the Beautiful Necessity" that imposes character on destiny. *Amor fati* becomes the proposition of a unity that is necessary because it constitutes subjectivity, and the affirmation of subjectivity is the right answer to the riddle of the Sphinx.

The Genius of The Heart

Nietzsche's enigmatic "genius of the heart" is the figure of Dionysian pessimism associated with *amor fati* in *The Gay Science*. Adrian del Caro identified the genius as Dionysus himself, so ambiguous is Nietzsche's designation.[14] At one moment, he is presented as "no less a one than the God Dionysus," (BGE 295) an equivocal statement that suggests he is Dionysus himself. But Nietzsche confronts his readers with the mysterious identity of the genius in his autobiography in a demand that they reconsider the passage in *Beyond Good and Evil* in which

---

12   "I hope it is somewhat better than whim at last, but we cannot spend the day in explanation." (Emerson, W 2:52).

13   Even with the "Imp of The Perverse," Poe's symbol of evil for evil's sake, the deliberate depravity of the narrator is exposed by his confession, provoked by a seemingly more uncontrollable sense of conscience.

14   Adrian Del Caro, *Nietzsche Contra Nietzsche: Creativity and The Anti-Romantic* (Baton Rouge and London: Louisiana State University Press, 1989): 229.

he claims not to have named the genius, thus his naming of Dionysus excludes the god from the list of possibles.

Nietzsche states that his genius is a "strange and precarious spirit" (BGE 295) whom he has encountered over the years: the foreign, excitable Emerson, whose books Nietzsche returned to over the course of his life, is quickly evoked. This image of Emerson persists: the spirit-god is called a "tempter/essayist," an "anchorite," and a "Pied Piper of conscience," (295) terms that immediately describe Emerson as Nietzsche saw him. Nietzsche wrote that what is most prominent about the genius is his ability to seduce and be seduced: he knows his audience. The genius seduces by "the art of seeming," (295) a complicated orientation to appearances, simplified as the approximation of subject and object that is resistant to language, nonetheless issued through the kinds of words that "bind us to him" (295). The genius knows just what to say and what not to say. He has plumbed the depths and reached the surface. He understands the illusory nature of "Being," and has become part of it by virtue of his affirmation.

The chief appeal of the genius is his astonishing negativity: his claim that he would like to make humankind "better… and more evil" (295) completely seduces Nietzsche. Emerson's conception of a morality that debased evil from the absolute power that Christianity granted it confirmed Nietzsche's project to construct a morality *Beyond Good and Evil*. He prized Emerson's revaluation of evil, mostly for its honesty.

An honest evaluation of evil also reevaluates what is good, and this is exactly what Emerson as "the genius of the heart" offered to Nietzsche. The potential of the genius is grounded in a benevolence that belongs to nature. Nietzsche considered this idealism in *The Gay Science*, especially at the end of Book Five, where he reflected on "the ideal of a human, superhuman well-being and benevolence" (382) as a figure of the coming philosophy. He called this a "peculiar, seductive, and dangerous ideal" (382) because of its reliance on the temperament of its beholder: cheerfulness is required. Cheerfulness is an attribute of "the great health" that Nietzsche described in the preface to *Human All Too Human* as the condition of accepting illusion. His "formula for greatness" begins to look like a formula for happiness, except that it recommends pessimism rather than optimism and joy over contentment. Its chief strength and danger is a kind of silliness that flouts gravitational force, effecting a saltatory philosophy, the kind Nietzsche recommends in *Will to Power* (1038).

Emerson, as a self-proclaimed "Professor of the Joyous Science," made the claim in "The Scholar" that Nietzsche took up in *The Gay Science*: philosophy should be the art of the poet-professor. Nietzsche's statement that the pedagogical effect of the scholar should "should inspire, elevate, and encourage" his readers "to be virtuous" (381) reflects Emerson's "Joyous Science," (p. 252) which specifically refers to teaching as a way to affirm the future. Although Nietzsche's virtue is equivocal, his moral emphasis was bona fide. Emerson's virtue was as equivocal: his aim was not to become virtuous, rather, to become virtue itself by way of a physiological event that permits the moral sentiment in nature to speak. The figure of the genius represents *amor fati* by way of a claim to poetic language that issues from a kind of benevolence that resembles the scales of justice. Nietzsche's dancing philosopher is like *Zarathustra's* tightrope man, balancing on the edge of meaninglessness, stabilized by a positive force that produces a new—aesthetic or emotional—subjectivity. Whether or not such subjectivity as a formula for character can be taught is open to question.

In order to accept the postulate of this kind of subjectivity, one must find "Where the good begins" (GS 53). To discern "the land of goodness," one's vision must be blurred: "the duller the eye, the more extensive the good," as if viewed from a distance (53). This enervated vision, shared by "common people and children," who lack the "bad conscience" (53) of the great thinkers, keeps one cheerful. Nietzsche did not mean to devalue this way of seeing. Visual synthesis is also an aspect of the "subject-unity" explained in *Will to Power* (490), wherein a commander's willful ignorance is required for proper leadership. "Bad conscience" is its particularly dangerous aspect: how can one presume to perform "virtue," exactly as one realizes one's "drive to evil," (53) or in the case of the commander, of one's knowledge of the incriminating details? A kind of suspension of disbelief is needed, perhaps one that is native to the uneducated.

Emerson's perspective prescribes self-trust: with the courage of enthusiasm, one reaffirms benevolence in nature. This is the logic of the "intellectual nomad," the character Emerson introduces in "History," for whom "all things are sacred, beautiful and true" (p. 12).

Nietzsche took this as the epigraph to *The Gay Science*, indicating that the entire book was preoccupied with a kind of magical seeing, an orientation to appearances in which the subject is not only relative to the object but becomes it, and by this process, endures the self-over-coming of the thinker plagued by "bad conscience" (53). Even so, the moment of light when the thinker sees himself in the other is "the art of seeming," a seduction that Nietzsche resists.

In Nietzsche's reasoning, to accept appearances as real is to delude oneself necessarily. To accept the sovereignty of oneself, at least physically, is a benevolent bluff constructed by the visual synthesis of a commanding "subject-unity". Loving this illusion is not necessary, but with *amor fati*, Nietzsche recommends it. His "genius of the heart" represents a fierce kind of love, composed in part of hate, that reckons with the beloved, whether the beloved is woman, humankind or oneself.

Ariadne

The idea that *amor fati* is self-directed is available in the translation of the term as love of one's fate. But fate for Nietzsche and Emerson always incorporates the other. This is what Ariadne has to do with *amor fati*: Nietzsche's linking what he called the riddle of Ariadne with a justification of life by way of an affirmation of the multiplicity is the moment when *amor fati* becomes more than one. *Amor fati* is not simply love of one's own fate, but love of the complex.

Ariadne represents Nietzsche's vision of the female ideal that Emerson proposes in "Heroism" and Nietzsche developed in "Women and their action at a distance" (GS 60). In Nietzsche's evaluation of Emerson's heroine, he presents women magically hovering on the surface and kept at a distance, indicating that her threat was essential to her power in the conditions of gender warfare whose belligerence expresses love. As a psychological figure, Nietzsche's woman is strongest as a fuzzy projection, like the illusions of unity, subjectivity, and Being. As with the ideal of "Being," Ariadne is affirmed in the service of great health. She is kept at a distance for the same reason that Nietzsche would keep anything sacred at a distance, like the mountain that loses its significance once scaled. While Emerson sought a physical apprehension of the divine, Nietzsche was satisfied with its metaphysical aspect. He seemed to require this kind of idealism in his thinking, especially regarding woman, a figure he mostly disdains unless she is the bride of Dionysus.

Circles

The one woman that Nietzsche loved was the emblem of eternity. His bride was the heavy prospect of eternal return, whose "extreme fatalism" could only be endured by "enjoyment of all kinds of uncertainty," which required "abolition of the 'will'," (WP 1060) a kind of willingness to play the game. "The joy of the circle" (1067) is the process of this game. Nietzsche's metaphor of the circle regarding his ideation of eternal return appears to have come directly from Emerson's essay "Circles," in which the "eternal generation of circles" (p. 318) encompasses the physical, sociological and philosophical power of *amor fati*.

Muted references to "Circles' ' occur throughout "Schopenhauer as Educator," where Nietzsche expresses an ethics of activism regarding the "circle of duties" (5) of the philosopher. He embraces Schopenhauer's pessimism, but criticizes the character of his philosophy, specifically his lack of love (3). The philosopher's obligation is to mitigate the sufferings in life, rather than deny them: Schopenhauer's nihilism was rejected in favor of the creative, physical philosophy that Nietzsche found in Emerson.

Woman

There are moments in *The Gay Science* when Nietzsche equates the value of woman with the value of life and the exalted love of friendship. But in *Beyond Good and Evil* and *Ecce Homo*, his acidic provocations peel layer after layer of the surface woman, as a kind of training to produce thicker skin, it seems, as if to hone the will of his future female reader. His provocation performs the passionate engagement of a self-professed warrior whose martial style, modelled after Sallust, implicated all the craft of warfare, including the consumption of its enemy.

Gilles Deleuze asserted that Ariadne was an aspect of Nietzsche's anima, using Jung's term.[15] Jung's anima was deliberately vague: the manifold images of Mother/Beloved compose the archetype of femaleness as conceived by the son.[16] Jung believed that Nietzsche lacked anima; Del Caro argued that he suppressed it.[17] Connected with his reading of Emerson, Nietzsche did not reject anima but projected it into his writing where it appears both in the form of the Sphinx as a protector of the arcane, and as Ariadne, acting tentatively as the eternal feminine. In the form of the Sphinx, the presence of woman provokes catastrophe; as Ariadne, she inspires the formation of a star in the process of Nietzsche's consideration. Anima in this sense is always essential to his thought. As a projection of the Sphinx, his anima expresses his will to deconstruct morality. As a projection of the eternal feminine, Nietzsche's anima is the enigma of *amor fati*.

Nietzsche's excavation of the symbolic within his performance in the multiplicity is more similar to Emerson's Oversoul than it is to his Overman in conjunction with his consideration of woman. Nietzsche's pattern, to use Jung's term, was this process of excavation. He wrote in his autobiography that he is dynamite; his thinking employed the explosive element of passionate attachment. We encounter the detritus of Nietzsche's psyche in his notorious reckoning with woman. It is almost as if his philosophical inquiries yielded the rhetorical violence of one afflicted with Tourette's syndrome. But Nietzsche's intentions were not inexplicit: he treated symbolic woman according to the personal ethic described in the preface to *Zarathustra*: "Oh my soul, I taught you the despising that does not come like a worm-eating, the great, the loving contempt that loves most, where it despises most" (58). In the same way that Nietzsche's ideal man was the Overman, Ariadne is Nietzsche's Overwoman: together, they make

---

15   Gilles Deleuze, *Nietzsche and Philosophy* (New York, Columbia University Press, 1983): 177-188.

16   Carl Gustave Jung, *The Collected Works of C.G. Jung, Volume IX*, trans. R.F.C. Hull (Princeton, NJ: Princeton University Press, 1951): 12-17.

17   Adrian Del Caro, review of Paul Bishop, *The Dionysian Self: C. G. Jung's Reception of Friedrich Nietzsche, in The Journal of Nietzsche Studies* (Berlin and New York: Walter de Gruyter,1995).

an Oversoul. Whereas Nietzsche's "woman as such" is represented by the Sphinx, who threatens men by "the incomprehensibleness, extent, and deviation of her desires and virtues," (BGE 239) Ariadne represents acquiescence. As an idealized figure who is literally created by affirmation, she is language at its most enchanting.

With the symbols of the Sphinx and Ariadne, we have philosophy situated alternately in the labyrinth or on the mountain path at Thebes: violence against the philosopher is promised in both situations. The Sphinx brings us crashing back to the earth, while Ariadne presents as a sidereal force to guide us through the labyrinth. The point is made in Del Caro's in "Symbolizing Philosophy: Ariadne and The Labyrinth": Ariadne represents our ability to overcome the abyssal space of passive nihilism in which the philosopher is destined to be lost. For the Dionysian philosopher, Ariadne symbolizes the inspired sword/word of the thread/narrative that conducts the philosopher through the labyrinth. The philosopher must make her own meanings as she proceeds, interpreting herself by the constellation of "Being," becoming with each experience. Emerson's invocation of the "fair girl" makes this resolution plausible for the female reader. The littoral figure is welcomed as a real, politically-charged participant in the negotiation of "Being". This is not the case with Nietzsche: he preferred his women to remain at sea.

Nietzsche's insistence that woman should appear silently enchanted is uttered in the same breath as his statement that the most powerful women "had just to thank their force of will—and not their schoolmasters—for their power and ascendancy over men" (GS 68). This is one of the few instances that he praises a woman's will. The pedagogical message expressed in the "Will and Willingness" aphorism directs the coming philosophy to educate women to become more like Napoleon's mother, i.e., willful, even as Nietzsche later admonishes them: "*mulieres taceat* in politics!" (BGE 232) The dynamic of his polemics regarding women provokes his female readers to empower themselves.

Part I.

SPHINX

One Mouth

Nietzsche had lost his cherished copy of George Fabricius' translation of Emerson's *Essays: First Series* in a Swiss train station in the summer of 1874 when his suitcase containing it was stolen. He quickly invested in another, which he read again with intensity: the remaining copy contains Nietzsche's passionate notations. There are many exclamation points, fewer question marks, much underlining and single, double and triple lines in different shades of ink and pencil alongside Emerson's text. His marginalia variously express affirmation, consideration, rejection and acceptance of Emerson's thinking, illuminating a process that should inform any interpretation of Nietzsche's work.

Nietzsche felt an affinity with Emerson: he called him his "twin soul" (KSA 9:6 [477]). This note in particular, which was later versified verbatim in "Dionysian Dithyrambs" and published at the end of *The Gay Science*, describes his intimacy with the American essayist:

> Here you sit, relentless as my curiosity, which compelled me to you: well, Sphinx, I am an interrogator, like you: this abyss is common to us-it is possible that we talked with one mouth (KSA 9:13 [22]).

The placement of the note—on an endpaper of his *Versuche* among other responses to the book—indicates that the "you" Nietzsche meant to address was Emerson, with whom he imagined sharing "one mouth." Clearly, speaking with the same mouth means saying the same thing

Nietzsche's diction in the note echoes the ancient riddle: "What is that which has one mouth and yet becomes four-footed and two-footed and three-footed?"[18] "One mouth" resonates the correct answer: Man. The image that Nietzsche presents of the poet-philosopher as part human and part beast elucidates his notion of man as a divided and puzzling object to himself. His designation of Emerson as

---

18   Apollodorus Apollodorus, *The Library*, trans. Sir James George Frazer (Cambridge, MA: Harvard University Press, 1921).

the Sphinx and his self-identification with it imply that he understood Emerson as asking the same questions that he asked, which means that he understood that the problems of his own philosophy were the same as the problems of Emerson's.

While Emerson is appreciated as a rhapsodic writer— he positively gushes— Nietzsche is esteemed more simply as a rhapsode, the kind that appears in Sophocles' Oedipus cycle. The poet, puzzler and philosopher are confused in this image, and that is the point. The "truth" is not had by any one of these characters; the enigma is everything. Nietzsche's aphorisms are not so much reductions as they are puzzles themselves: there is usually a question and an attempt at an answer that does not close the question but cuts through it. Emerson's essays are likewise open, containing fertile inquiries that seed burgeoning if discursive attempts to reckon with metaphysical questions in the absence of a traditional, unified metaphysics. If God is dead, as both writers claimed—with some hedging from Emerson, "as if God were dead—" (W 1:134) what are we?

The instability of the human condition is symbolized by the Sphinx as a menace to humanity. The inability to find a central meaning in existence condemns one to mental suffering. Francis Bacon provided an avid description in "The Sphinx or Science": questions arise, and "unless they be solved and disposed of, they strangely torment and worry the mind, pulling it first this way and then that, and fairly tearing it to pieces" causing "distraction and laceration of mind".[19] In this condition, how can we avoid the vertigo of "the widening gyre," the dread summoned by Yeats' Sphinx? Like the death of a star, the loss of being—a steady spot on the unstable grounds of succession—threatens the order of the cosmos and everything in it.

Blessed Unity

In Emerson's essay, "History," he recounts the ancient fable: "the Sphinx… was said to sit in the road-side and put riddles to every passenger. If the man could not answer, she swallowed him alive" (p.

---

19   Francis Bacon, "Sphinx or Science." In *Of the Wisdom of the Ancients* XX-VIII, 1857.

32). Earlier in the essay, he identified the riddle as our interpretations of ourselves: "This human mind wrote history, and this must
read it. The Sphinx must solve her own riddle" (p. 4). In Nietzsche's
notations, he underlined "If the man could not answer," and at the
bottom of the page, he wrote:

> There is much to be answered when an enigma is given up, and
> to believe that it has been solved-the sphinx has sometimes
> fallen down with the courage to answer the riddle of life (KSA
> 9:17 [18]).

The metaphysical "enigma" that had been "given up" was replaced in
"History" by self-determination. For Nietzsche, the supposition that
the mystery of the human condition could be solved, especially in this
solipsistic fashion, was affirmed at the peril of the questioner whose
courage alone could undo him.

For Emerson, the metaphor of the Sphinx explicitly signified
"the perception of identity" that "unites all things" (W 9:412).[20] This
perception was associated with the vision of a beneficent nature that
inspires an appreciation of "Being". In his essay "Fate," he exhort-
ed his readers to accept the "Blessed Unity," which he also called the
"Beautiful Necessity" (p. 48). Nietzsche, who was immersed in his re-
reading of Emerson during the time he was composing *Thus Spake
Zarathustra*, seems to allude to the "Blessed Unity" in his "On the Vision and the Riddle:" a shepherd swallows most of a black snake, bites
off its head, and spits it out. The unity is temporary, but his transformation occurs nonetheless. He becomes a Yes-sayer.

In *amor fati*, Nietzsche's fallen Sphinx recovers as a courageous
questioner whose affirmation of the riddle of life modeled Emerson's.
He became a Yes-sayer to the "Beautiful Necessity," an illusion of uni-

---

20   Edward Emerson's note reads in full "Mr. Emerson wrote in his notebook in 1859: "I have often been asked the meaning of the 'Sphinx.' It is this,—
The perception of identity unites all things and explains one by another, and the
most rare and strange is equally facile as the most common. But if the mind live
only in particulars, and see only differences (wanting the power to see the whole—
all in each), then the world addresses to this mind a question it cannot answer, and
each new fact tears it in pieces, and it is vanquished by the distracting variety." (W
9:412)

ty that conjures the whole in the eternal balancing of its parts. Both writers understood that the nature of humankind was metaphysical: it is always a little beyond itself. Being beyond oneself is another way of saying ecstatic. Nietzsche, after all, identified an immovable force: "joy accompanies...joy does not move" (WP 688). Happiness in its classic form of *eudaimonia* is described as a state of consciousness that is achieved through fusion with power. The will to power is countered by the willingness of *amor fati*, whose condition is not happiness, but joy, an emotional integrity inspired by Emerson.[21]

Secret of Nature

The Sphinx in the Greek myth is associated with the blindness of Oedipus. According to Sophocles' version, Oedipus, ravaged by the shame of having killed his father and married his mother, and repentant after his mother/wife's subsequent suicide, sticks pins in his eyes and blinds himself. This is one of many myths in which man's attempt to avoid his fate by evading projected circumstances leads him right to it. The message of these myths is that humans cannot overpower nature by the acquisition of special information: Oedipus' attempts to overcome his fate failed.

Emerson and Nietzsche agree that the Sphinx represents the secret of nature, but they characterized nature differently. For Emerson, nature represents the unity of interconnection. One cannot discern meaning in a sea of individual iterations—each particular presents a puzzle on its own—but the understanding of nature as interconnectivity permits interpretation. For Nietzsche, nature is a sorceress whose ways ought not be revealed, except perhaps once, in the *vita femina* (GS 339). Though the Sphinx in Emerson's eponymous poem is distinctly

---

21   Another of Nietzsche's notes connects his affirmation of life with the Overman, inspired by Emerson's Oversoul: "Apparently while working on Zarathustra, Nietzsche, in a moment of despair, said in one of his notes: 'I do not want life again. How did I endure it? Creating. What makes me stand the sight of it? The vision of the overman who affirms life. I have tried to affirm it myself-alas!'" Friedrich Nietzsche, quoted in Kaufmann, *The Gay Science with A Prelude in Rhymes and An Appendix of Songs*, trans. Walter Kaufmann (New York: Random House, 1974), 19.

maternal, he did not imagine the figure as exclusively feminine. In his journal, he described the Egyptian Sphinx as an androgynous creature whose "complacency and tranquility" are an "an expression of health" (7:62). Nietzsche's Sphinx is decidedly female, of Greek heritage, a more damaging version than the auspicious Egyptian figure.

In the *Nachlass*, Nietzsche's Sphinx is associated with seduction:

> The beautiful is a smile of nature, an excess of strength and a pleasure in sensations... the virgin body of the sphinx. The purpose of the beautiful is seduction to life. Essentially, what is that smile, that fascination? Negative: the concealment of necessity, the smoothing out of all wrinkles, and the serene glance of the soul of things (7:143-144).

The smoothing gesture and spiritualized aspect of the Sphinx clearly depict nature as nurture, but Nietzsche's characterization condemns the nurturing virgin as a deceptive seductrix. This confusion of the maternal with the erotic precipitates the reversal of the ideal female, one for which Pierre Hadot[22] finds a possible influence in Goethe, whose verse from Faust conflates respect with terror:

> Respect the mystery
> Let not your eyes give in to lust
> nature the Sphinx, A monstrous thing
> Will terrify you with her innumerable breasts.[23]

Goethe's Sphinx is unlike Emerson's gregarious creature: nature is horrific, and exponentially female. Hadot likens this Sphinx to Baubo, the bawdy goddess of mirth to whom the revised version of *The Gay Science* was dedicated. Nietzsche's Baubo is mediated by the charm of her humor and will to console, but Goethe's is just a "monstrous thing" whose nurturing powers threaten to make of man a pig.

---

22   Pierre Hadot, *The Veil of Isis: An Essay on the History of the Idea of Nature*, trans. Michael Chase (Boston: Harvard University Press, 2008), 294.

23   Ibid.

Nietzsche's feminine Sphinx can be interpreted as an image of the emasculation of the blonde beast: the might of the lion is subdued by the meekness that the female head. As Kaufmann pointed out, the emasculation is associated with Christianity's need for the "extirpation of the impulses"[24]. The Sphinx dissuades our hero from action: as Circe, she turns men into greedy, oblivious animals, unable to discern. The nobility of the body is eradicated by her intoxications and paralysis ensues.

While Emerson's Sphinx is meant to represent a vision of unity, Nietzsche's Sphinx is a metaphor for duplicity. In *Beyond Good and Evil*, Plato is given as example: his "sphinx-nature" is expressed in his sleeping with a copy of Aristophanes under his pillow, rather than a more sacred text (28). Platonic truth is always betrayed by humorous hypocrisy or deliberate deception. As "the tempter," this Sphinx presents nothing true in its variations of truth as such. This figure appears in the first aphorism of the book, asking "strange, wicked, questionable questions":

> Is it any wonder that we should finally become suspicious, lose patience, and turn away impatiently? That we should finally learn from this Sphinx to ask questions, too? *Who* is it really that puts questions to us here? *What* in us really wants "truth"? (1) (Nietzsche's emphasis).

Questioning the value of the will to truth dismantles the ideal, as the questions themselves are dismantled in "a rendezvous of questions and question marks" (1). The metaphor of the Sphinx in this instance invokes the Greek ideal of the potency of the human in nature as a protector of the arcane. Nietzsche's self-identification with the creature suggests that the Greek animation of the riddle of life composed his understanding of himself.

One of the ancient Greek ways of knowing was by way of oracles— what we might understand as a kind of magic—in a world enchanted by nature. What sort of magic did Nietzsche suggest is a way to knowledge? His complicity with language permitted him to claim many truths and no truths at the same time. Like Arthur Rimbaud with

---

24   Kaufmann, *Nietzsche*, 225.

his "*magique étude de bonheur*,"[25] Nietzsche proposed a subversion of dogmatic ontologies to reveal Heraclitan hermeneutics in which meaning is never resolved but emits from constant play between opposites.

Emerson's Sphinxes

The symbol of the Sphinx was important for Emerson. He had Sphinx figurines, a Sphinx doorknob, and his poem, "The Sphinx," was his favorite.[26] In her interpretation of the poem, Laura Dassow Walls relates his titular metaphor to the titular metaphor of Bacon's essay, "The Sphinx or Science". The Sphinx that appears in Emerson's poem, however, is not a symbol of material science, but of the psychological nature of man, a distinction that Bacon establishes.[27] Over the course of Emerson's journal entries, the Sphinx begins as enigma, persists as the menace of systematic thinking and resolves as resolution itself: the riddle of human nature cannot be solved by science; indeed, it cannot be solved at all but mediated in our attempts to unriddle it.

The figure first appears in Emerson's journal by way of Germaine de Staël. Starting in 1823 as a student at the Cambridge Divinity School, he devoured De Staël's works, from which he copied the phrase: "The enigma of ourselves swallows up like the sphinx thousands of systems which pretend to the glory of having guessed

---

25   Arthur Rimbaud, "O Saisons! O Chateau!" in *Illuminations*, translated by Louise Varèse (New York: New Directions Publishing,1886).

26   Quoted in Laura Dassow Walls, *Emerson's Life in Science: The Culture of Truth* (Cornell: Cornell University Press, 2003), 29.

27   The two kinds of Sphinx-riddles that Bacon delineates generate two kinds of power provided they are solved. In each case, the correct solution grants command over the category. While the scientist's riddle concerned the nature of things, whose solution gained "the command over things natural,—over bodies, medicines, mechanical powers, and infinite other of the kind—... the one proper and ultimate end of true natural philosophy," Oedipus' riddle concerned the nature of man, whose solution earned him prophetic powers: "for whoever has a thorough insight into the nature of man may shape his fortune almost as he will, and is born for empire." Francis Bacon, "The Sphinx or Science," Chapter XXVIII, 1857.

its meaning" (2:121).[28]   The meaning of such glory is summed up in Cornel West's evaluation of Emerson, in which he described the drive of academic philosophy as the "quest for certainty and its hope for professional, i.e., scientific respectability".[29] But such correctness was not the validation that Emerson sought. He had deliberately removed himself from the academy when he quit his official ministry positions in Boston and moved to Concord to begin a career as a freelance lecturer in the newly popular circuits of the Lyceum movement. This rejection of respectability was intensified by his delivery of the now famous "Divinity School Address," a bold critique of the spiritual flaccidity of the Boston Brahmins. As Richard Deming wrote, Emerson did "not wish to engage the necessary conventions of systematic or academic philosophy…. [his] efforts are directed towards combining philosophy and poetry in an attempt to engage the problem of systematic thinking".[30] His lack of "strict discipline," (KSB 6:566) as Nietzsche phrased it, earned Emerson a place in "the genteel tradition" in American letters as an earnest dialectician whose essays resonated where his poems did not.

Emerson's criticism of systematic thinking was outlined in his journal's next encounter with the Sphinx. On August 1, 1835, he cited his brother Charles, a Greek scholar, in the context of Guilliame Oegger's manifesto of Christian mysticism:

> There sits the Sphinx from age to age, in the road, Charles says, and every wise man that comes by has a crack with her. But this Oegger's plan and scope argue great boldness and manhood, to depart thus widely from all routine and seek to put his hands, like Atlas, under nature, and heave her from her rest. Why the world exists, and that it exists for a language or

---

28   Germaine de Staël, *On Germany*, quoted in *Journals of Ralph Waldo Emerson, With Annotations*, ed. Edward Waldo Emerson and Waldo Emerson Forbes (New York and Boston: Houghton Mifflin), 121.

29   Cornell West, *The American Evasion of Philosophy: A Genealogy of Pragmatism* (Madison: The University of Wisconsin Press,1989), 36.

30   Richard Demming, "Reading, Agency, and The Question of 'Fate'," in *Listening on All Sides: Towards an Emersonian Ethics of Reading* (Standford: Stanford University Press, 2007), 62.

medium whereby God may speak to man, this is his query, this his answer (3:525).

In this entry, Emerson invokes Oegger's Swedenborgian system of correspondences along with an image of Atlas, the mortal behind nature who controls it. Though he was enthusiastic about Oegger's ideas, which presented a complex scheme of God in nature,[31] he was wary of Oegger's orthodoxy. Later in his journal, he criticized its implications:

> I find good things in this manuscript of Oegger, and I am taken with the design of his work. But it seems as if everybody was insane on one side, and the Bible makes them as crazy as Bentham or Spurzheim or politics. The ethical doctrines of these theosophists are true and exalting, but straightway they run upon their Divine Transformation, the Death of God, etc., and become horn-mad. To that point they speak reason, then they begin to babble, and so this man cries out, Wo to them that do not believe, etc., etc. This obstinate Orientalism that God is a petty Asiatic king and will be very angry (5:505).

The combination of an apprehension of God with a dogmatic sociological application seemed to him like thuggery. Although Oegger's philosophy was not dissimilar to Emerson's—language and nature are sacred—Emerson's conception of the divine human confused the system. If we are not God's subordinate but coordinate, then nature is not only God's playground, but also ours.

Pistareen-Providence

The question of whether Emerson himself was guilty of such thuggery is illuminated by West's exposition of his damaging forays

---

31   Guillaume Caspar Lecroy Oegger, professor of philosophy, and vicar of Notre Dame in Paris in the early 1830's, wrote *Le vrai Messie : ou l'Ancien et le Nouveau Testament examinés d'après les principes de la langue de la nature*, from which Emerson copied pages into his journal in August 1835 (from Eliza Peabody's translations).

into ethnology.[32]   Emerson disseminated the ugly images of the new science of race via his derogation of the Irish and Negro, but his conclusion that "if you have Man, black or white is an insignificance" (W 11:145) denies the dogma of race-based valuations. Nonetheless, one finds a white supremacist lurking in an early journal, where Emerson compares the black men he encountered on the streets of Cambridge to elephants (1:48). As Peter Fields points out, Emerson's opinions regarding those of African descent shifted over the course of his career, beginning in patrician discrimination and ending in passionate abolitionism.[33]   But Fields is wrong when he claimed that Emerson's thinking was restricted by the idealism of white supremacy.

Emerson was influenced by his friend Louis Agassiz, the Swiss-American physician whose studies in zoology and botany impressed him, but he disdained Agassiz's polygenist ideology in the same way that he dismissed phrenology and other forms of pseudo-science:

I know the mental proclivity of physicians. I hear the chuckle of the phrenologists. Theoretic kidnappers and slave-drivers, they esteem each man the victim of another, who winds him round his finger by knowing the law of his being; and, by such cheap signboards as the color of his beard or the slope of his occiput, reads the inventory of his fortunes and character (W 3:54).

Emerson's distrust of the racial taxonomies of his day disentangled him from the newly fashionable tenets of white supremacy whose theories he rejected. He did not privilege whiteness; his disparagement of the Irish and Germans suggests otherwise.[34] Neither was he convinced

---

32   West, *American Evasion, 28-34.*

33   Peter S. Fields, "The Strange Career of Emerson and Race," *American Nineteenth Century History* 2 (2001):1-32.

34   Nell Irvin Painter writes about Emerson as a Saxonist but states plainly that "Emerson makes it crystal clear that "Saxon" (or, later, "Anglo-Saxon") is not a synonym for "white,"even though the historiographical literature often seems to equate them." Painter, Nell Irvin. "Ralph Waldo Emerson's Saxons." The Journal of American History, vol. 95, no. 4, 2009, pp. 977–985. JSTOR, www.jstor.org/stable/27694556. Accessed 18 July 2021.

of the superiority of the Anglo Saxons. Despite his excessive enthusiasm for the manliness of the English uber-tribe, he remained aloof. As he wrote in a letter to Margaret Fuller Ossoli: "My respect is the more generous that I have no sympathy with him, only an admiration".[35]

His multiracial vision of the new world extended "to every race and skin, white men, red men, yellow men, black men" (W 11:542). Russell Goodman uses the term racialism, not racism, to distinguish Emerson's ethnology from bigotry.[36]

Emerson articulated his theory of race in *English Traits*, a long encomium on the virtues of the English, in his aptly entitled essay, "Race." Even as he asserted the "immortal" power of race, he degraded it: "the barriers of race are not so firm" (p. 51). He wrote that "credence" and "civilization" counteract the fatalism of race, using the English as example (pp. 49-50). Most of the "Race" section describes the multiracial origins of Londoners, whom he likens to cement: "water, lime and sand make mortar, so certain temperaments marry well, and, by well-managed contrarieties, develop as drastic a character as the English" (p. 52). Earlier in his journal, he had proposed a similar chemical destiny regarding the promise of North Americans:

> [A]s in the old burning of the Temple at Corinth, by the melting and intermixture of silver and gold and other metals a new compound more precious than any, called Corinthian brass, was formed; so in this continent, – asylum of all nations, – the energy of Irish, Germans, Swedes, Poles, and Cossacks, and all the European tribes, – of the Africans, and of the Polynesians, – will construct a new race, a new religion, a new state, a new

---

35   Though he esteemed the Saxon aspect of the English temperament as the most "manly," he wrote in a letter to Margaret Fuller Ossoli regarding the Anglo Saxon: "My respect is the more generous that I have no sympathy with him, only an admiration." At the end of *English Traits*, he delivered his final evaluation of the Anglo Saxons: "They are slow and reticent, and are like a dull good horse which lets every nag pass him, but with whip and spur will run down every racer in the field. They are right in their feeling, though wrong in their speculation." (W 5:307)

36   Russell B. Goodman, *American Philosophy Before Pragmatism* (United Kingdom: Oxford University Press, 2015), 191.

literature, which will be as vigorous as the new Europe which came out of the smelting-pot of the Dark Ages (7:115).

His idealism of intermixing tribes was simplified publicly a decade later in the observation that "you cannot draw the line where a race begins or ends" (p. 45). Emerson refuted the dogma of racial purity—"Though we flatter the self-love of men and nations by the legend of pure races, all our experience is of the gradation and resolution of races—" (p. 50) and advanced the estimation that "the best nations are those most widely related; and navigation, as effecting a world-wide mixture, is the most potent advancer of nations" (p. 51). Clearly, the imperialism of the English promised a new-world "smelting-pot".

But this grand destiny was mitigated by what Emerson calls "pistareen-Providence," in which "there is complicity, expensive races,—race living at the expense of race" (W 5:7). The same contradiction between freedom and its lack featured in "Fate" polarized his conception of race, which he deemed, like temperament, a natural determinant. As Goodman observed, Emerson seemed to cede to the preponderance of fate regarding race in his *Conduct of Life* essays, where he effectively caricatured one unfortunate tribe after another.[37] Rather than directly confronting the problem of slavery in these works, which were written when his abolitionism was increasing in intensity, the operating condition of the new world was effectively swept under the rug, or rather, under the edges of Emerson's irony. "Pistareen" is clearly meant to disparage the Christian ideal of divine Providence that applied only to wealthy white men.

The end of "Fate" makes it plain that Emerson did not recommend such providence. He published the essay in 1860, a decade after the Fugitive Slave Law was enacted. The conflict between fate and freedom had been temporarily resolved by the law, which made all Americans complicit in the system of slavery. The bitterness he felt for his own race was self-directed in his journal: "The absence of moral feeling in the white man is the very calamity I deplore. The captivity of thousands of Negroes is nothing to me" (11:385).[38] This irony comes across

---

37   Ibid.

38   That this 1851 journal entry was followed by a searing critique of Daniel

in "Fate" as ambivalence, weighted towards the necessity of action. If we must accept our circumstances, we must also propel ourselves into "the spirit of the times" (p. 5). "The power of character" insists that we cannot but perform ourselves in the world. Much of the beginning of the essay describes an intense tribal or religious fatalism that terminates the individual will: "organization tyrannizing character" (p. 9). But the direct message of his earlier essays, "Self Reliance," (1841) and "On the Anniversary of the Emancipation of the Negroes in the British West Indies," (1844) preached an ethic of self-determination: "I say to you, you must save yourself, black or white, man or woman" (p. 325). This ethic is emphasized in the final words of "Fate:" the law of the "Beautiful Necessity" accounts for and counts on "the pure in heart to draw on all its omnipotence" (p. 50).[39] The need for activism overrides the "Blessed Unity" of fatalism.

Emerson's vision of the new world sought "to establish morality as the basis of all legislation," (W 11:310) imposing conscience as corrective. Though he was loath to perform as the foolish philanthropist whose self-satisfaction only maintained the status quo, he involved himself actively by writing letters of advocacy and presenting abolitionist lectures. In addition to his public antislavery statements, he boycotted local institutions that excluded blacks, as Frederick Douglass attested in his *Life and Times:*

Webster's immoral authority in the Compromise of 1850, which begins: "Webster truly represents the American people just as they are, with their vast material interests, their materialized intellects and low morals," (11:385) indicates what was on Emerson's mind at the time, supporting the interpretation that the register of his "captivity" entry was deliberately ironic.

39   In Edward Emerson's note on the final sentence of "Fate," he cites Emerson's 1852 notes and 1859 journal entry to elucidate his father's stance on the contrast between fate and freewill, which can be summarized by the following points excerpted from Emerson's journal:
1.The belief in Fate is unwholesome and can only be good where it teaches the strength of nature to man.
2.We only value a stroke of will; he alone is happy who has will; the rest are herds. He uses, they are used.
3.This will derives from the aboriginal nature, is perception of the eternal necessity. (W 6: 353)

[T]hough white and colored children attended the same schools and were treated kindly by their teachers, the New Bedford Lyceum refused till several years after my residence in that city to allow any colored person to attend the lectures delivered in its hall. Not until such men as Hon. Chas. Sumner, Theodore Parker, Ralph W. Emerson, and Horace Mann refused to lecture in their course while there was such a restriction was it abandoned (p. 261).

In his Emancipation speech, Emerson indirectly urged "the black race" to "contend with the white," to "strike in with effect and take a master's part in the music," claiming that "their more moral genius" was "indispensable" (146). Addressing a mostly white audience in Concord, Massachusetts in 1844—seven years before the enactment of the Fugitive Slave Act and seventeen years before the American Civil War—he proposed:

If the black man carries in his bosom an indispensable element of a new and coming civilization; for the sake of that element, no wrong nor strength nor circumstance can hurt him (p. 146).

He was clearly wrong on that account. Many black men were hurt, and still are hurt, by the legacy of slavery and its systemic devaluation of black life.

In The Name of Science

Emerson's conceit of the Sphinx extended in his journal towards a criticism of the error of the kind of systematic thinking that devalues the dignity of human life in all of its diversity. The Sphinx as an explicit metaphor for identity became an organizing principle that accounted for the cogency of the whole:
Facts abound
Rich
they come asking questions of us
This was what the fable of the Sphinx meant
And men are men of facts or men of principle

Facts ⟨fall on⟩ encumber men tyrannize & make the men of
routine[,] the men of understanding[,] the men of sense[,] but
if the man is true to his allegiance & insists on commanding[,]
dwells with the soul & sees the principle[,]then the facts fall
aptly into place[,] they know their master & the meanest of
them glorifies him (7:252).

The birth of modern science in the nineteenth century introduced
a glut of facts whose interpretation required a Tiresian wisdom that
the era's classifications of race denied. Newly popular race scientists
established the polygenist theory, in which the white races, specifically
the Anglo Saxons, were privileged as the fathers of civilization. The
dogma of white supremacy emerged from this view, promulgated
by ethnologists who favored the "civilized" European races over the
"uncivilized" Africans. Douglass criticized these theorists in a commencement speech delivered at Western Reserve College in 1854:

It is somewhat remarkable that, at a time when knowledge is
so generally diffused, when the geography of the world is so
well understood— when time and space, in the intercourse
of nations, are almost annihilated— when oceans have become bridges— the earth a magnificent ball— the hollow sky
a dome— under which a common humanity can meet in a
friendly conclave— when nationalities are being swallowed
up— and the ends of the earth brought together— I say it is
remarkable— nay, it is strange, that there should arise a pha-
lanx of learned men— speaking in the name of science— to
forbid the magnificent reunion of mankind in one brother-
hood. A mortifying proof is here given that the moral growth
of a nation, or an age, does not always keep pace with the
increase of knowledge, and suggests the necessity of means to
increase human love with human learning.[40]

Douglass's point was not dissimilar to Emerson's: the correct answer
to the riddle of the Sphinx is the love that binds humankind: "*Quan-*

---

40   Frederick Douglass papers at The Library of Congress: https://www.loc.
gov/item/mfd.49007/.

tus amor, tantus animus" (W 12:62) was Emerson's first principle. The problem, of course, is that the black man was not classified as a man. That Douglass made these observations in one of his many lectures meant to defend black humanity implicates racialism, even as its most innocuous, as merely a facet of racism, forged in the tenets of white supremacy.

Though Emerson was complicit in the casual distribution of racial stereotypes, he repudiated racialism as a method for determining the value of a human being. Luther Luedtke's proposition that "race science was a principal element in Emerson's metaphysics of history"[41] is simply untrue. In "History," the essay that was explicitly meant to establish the metaphysics of the Oversoul, he did not feature race but character. His naming of certain historical figures in the essay emphasized resistance to what he called in "Experience" "the contracting influence of so-called science" (p. 53). As the end of "History" declares, "the path of science and of letters is not the way into nature" (p. 41). These essays attest that the principle element in Emersonian metaphysics was moral rather than pseudo-scientific. Len Gougeon's conclusion best assesses Emerson's position regarding race:

> Ultimately, despite the prevalence of the "scientific" findings of his day, Emerson found theories of deterministic racial inferiority simply inconsistent "with [as Emerson put it] the principles on which the world is built," and he rejected all such theories outright.[42]

The legacy of polygenist theory created a monster: ethnological determinations rationalized genocide. Like Emerson, Nietzsche did not subscribe to white supremacy: his most frequent disparagements targeted women, Christians and Germans. But both writers have been read selectively by those interested in justifying race-based hate, despite their criticisms of systematic thinking.

---

41   Luther Luedtke, "Ralph Waldo Emerson Envisions the 'Smelting Pot'," MELUS 6, no. 2 (1979): 3–14.

42   Len Gougeon, "Militant Abolitionism: Douglass, Emerson, and the Rise of the Anti-Slave," The New England Quarterly 85, no. 4 (2012): 622–657.

Deep Disease

Nietzsche's reading of Emerson directly addressed his apprehension of the complexities of history regarding character. In one of his more enigmatic notes on the back cover of his *Versuche*, he wrote:

> These errors were necessary at this stage as a remedy; the education of the human race as a cure has a necessary and reasonable course.
> In this sense, I deny the necessity. It is fortuitous that this and that article of faith should be victorious. And especially! The result of the healing effect is very arbitrary, very unreasonable! Almost always a deep disease is the result of the new faith and not a cure! (KSA 9:13[1])

The obvious reference here is to Lessing's *The Education of The Human Race*. The note also seems to be related to Nietzsche's "Four Great Errors," in which he elaborates on the errors of causality. The question arises whether he thought the efforts of modern education were in vain.

A tentative answer is supplied In "Schopenhauer as Educator," where Nietzsche considered the problem of the generation of philosophy through education. If philosophical and religious thinking are replaced by another kind of idolatry, i.e., "the new faith," it will always be followed by a "deep disease". What is this "deep disease"? In the second section, Nietzsche answers this question:

> It is almost as obvious why a scholar must now become distorted and contorted - because he is supposed to be educated by science, that is to say by an inhuman abstraction - then one finally asks oneself: where are we, scholars and unscholarly, high placed and low, to find the moral exemplars and models among our contemporaries, the visible epitome of morality for our time?

He provides the same answer in the fourth section:

> He who regards his life as no more than a point in the evolution of a race or of a state or of a science; and thus regards himself as belonging wholly to the history of becoming, has not understood the lesson set him by existence and will have to learn it over again.

In a word, the "deep disease" was "scientificality," (BGE 208) the kind of systematic thinking that justified both slavery and the Third Reich. "Scientificality" is not a synonym for science as we know it, rather as Heidegger defined it in 1933: "Science is the questioning standing of one's ground in the midst of a constantly self-concealing totality of what is". This vague, self-involved abstraction is then complicated with nationalism: "Together, science and German destiny must come to power in the will to essence".[43] The rest, we know, is tragedy.

Neither Nietzsche nor Emerson was a nationalist, but they were both avid scientists, excited about new discoveries in the patterns of the natural world. Their questioning of the grounds themselves predicted relativity, and their focus on process proposed an experimentalism meant, in Nietzsche's words, "to guard and champion humanity, the inviolable sacred treasure gradually accumulated by the most various races" (4). Science in the service of humanity attempts to ameliorate its conditions, while "scientificality" involves tired bureaucratic thinking that disdains the whole even as it pretends to represent it. Nietzsche's problem with this was argued throughout his works, but in "Schopenhauer as Educator," the disease is associated with a lack of "moral exemplars." In featuring facts, we move away from poetry, as Emerson wrote. We attempt to control nature, not ourselves, as Bacon wrote. We do not quite answer the question of how to live. We are burdened by becoming.

In his note, Nietzsche affirmed chance, thereby denying the presence of reason in human progress. If the "new faith" in science merely replaced religion, we are left being commanded by a false idol. But Nietzsche affirmed the error of reasonable progress over arbitrary becoming in the beginning of "Schopenhauer as Educator":

---

43   Martin Heidegger, "The Self Assertion of The German University" in Martin Heidegger and National Socialism, ed. Gunther Neske & Emil Kettering (New York: Paragon House, 1990), 5-13.

We are responsible to ourselves for our own existence; consequently we want to be the true helmsman of this existence and refuse to allow our lives to resemble mindless acts of chance.

Nietzsche recommended that we take a "bold and dangerous line to this existence" and live by critical thinking as conscience. Though "education... as a cure" (KSA 9:13[1]) seems to justify the past, its focus on the future as a prospect for improvement affirms responsibility for its errors. A teacher has to take this axiom to teach. The "professors of the Joyous Science" meant to dignify the human spirit.

Transcendental Sphinx

The threshold poem of Emerson's first published volume of poetry, "The Sphinx," encapsulates ideas contained in *Nature*, "History," "Self Reliance" and "Nominalist and Realist." Emerson wrote the poem in 1841, around the time of the publication of *Essays: First Series*. There is no evidence that Nietzsche read it, but it is clear that he intuited the potency of its central metaphor.

"The Sphinx" in the poem is not the violent beast that Oedipus meets in the hills surrounding Thebes. Unlike his Sphinx from "History," Emerson's poetic Sphinx is maternal, brooding on "the meaning of man" in a nature driven by "animate poles". She contrasts the "unashamed" natural world with a humanity that "crouches and blushes," pronouncing that both are "by one music enchanted/by One deity stirred". Though she does not name the god, the Sphinx suggests that Eros is the "one deity," disguised as a "babe/.. bathed in joy" and described as "the sum of the world". The poem's Poet argues that becoming is the nature of the world, but he maintains that noumenal love organizes it. His identification of "love at the centre," and the "deep love that lieth under these pictures of time," provokes the Sphinx to ask, "Who has taught thee me to name?" indicating that she has heard the correct answer to her riddle. Her final words, "Who telleth one of my meanings/ Is master of all I am," are spoken "thorough a thousand voices:" she has become the "universal dame". Unlike the eternal feminine, the "universal dame" is earth-bound.

In its female form the Sphinx is usually savage and cruel: in Emerson's poem, however, she is a protectress of the illusion of unity. The Sphinx's diffusion at the end of the poem animates nature: she is incorporated into the various elements, illuminating them with her enigma to suggest, as Thomas Whittaker did, *Omnia exeunt in mysterium*.[44] The Sphinx's abrupt destruction implies that language is fugitive, as are matter and facts, and we cannot grasp them, or glimpse long in the flutter between transparent and opaque. As Emerson states plainly in his "Natural History of the Intellect":

> I believe in the existence of the material world as the expression of the spiritual or the real, and in the impenetrable mystery which hides (and hides through absolute transparency) the mental nature, I await the insight which our advancing knowledge of material laws shall furnish (p. 5).

These lines express the contradictions that compose our ability to interpret. They bring to mind the words of Emerson's disciple, Walt Whitman: "Strong upon me the life that does not exhibit itself, yet contains all the rest".[45]

The philosophical view in the poem marries Parmenidean being with Heraclitan becoming, affirming both what is and what is not in the same way that the Sphinx riddle affirms man in his various stages, that is, outside of the realm of becoming. The world of appearances, Parmenidean doxa, is understood as an aspect of truth, and therefore true. The Parmenidean ideal is represented by the Heraclitan real by way of a vision that blurs edges to see a whole. Change is made cogent by the beholder. The actual is apprehended by way of Apollonian "dry light;" (W 3:141) the real is perceived by Dionysian insight. Unity does not precipitate the singular vision; the singular vision precipitates unity.

---

44   Thomas Whittaker, "The Riddle of Emerson's 'Sphinx'," American Literature 27, no. 2 (May 1955): 179-195.

45   Walt Whitman, "Calamus: In Paths Untrodden," in Leaves of Grass (1867): 96.

The Writer

In "The Sphinx," the figures of the Poet and the writer of the poem are separate characters. The writer is audience to the Poet's exchange with the Sphinx: his role is to listen while they speak. As such, he is the Poet's poet, recording their interaction. The inclusion of the first person occurs only once, at the poem's center. This reticence indicates Emerson's stance outside the poet's frippery, the "clothed eternity" of his style that the Sphinx demeans as she frees herself from his yoke. While the gaze of the Poet inflicts nature with mood, the writer merely observes, appreciating the positive effects of the Poet's play with mythology. Most of the poem is dialogue, but the beginning and end are descriptions of the Sphinx, the writer's account of what he sees. She is at first a mocking and muddied creature, and at last a phenomena of natural beauty. Nature as a positive power, generated by the writer's auspicious vision, is the affirmation of the question posed in the poem regarding the unity of opposites as "primordial wholes".

The poem describes a nature in which opposites parry and harmonize. The Sphinx sounds like Heraclitus: her lines "Out of sleeping a waking, out of waking a sleep;/ life death overtaking" echo his fragment, "As the same thing in us are living and dead, waking and sleeping, young and old" (B88). The Poet also emphasizes opposites—pride and shame, joy and melancholy—but the unity of oppositions is ruined by man's idealism, which seeks to classify and conquer. These contradictions persist until the middle of the poem, where the Poet declares love as the bind. It seems that words gain propriety over the character who speaks them. As Heraclitus wrote, "It is wise to hearken not to me but to my word, and to confess that all things are one," (B 50) suggesting that he was simply a medium for a language that is numinous: "all things come to pass in accordance with this Word" (B2). A similar conception of language was outlined in Emerson's *Nature*, where we begin to understand his radical ideas.

Emerson's mysticism was prevalent, but it was not an alibi for unrelenting fatalism. West's assessment that Emerson's "mystical element...stands in stark contrast to his dominant Heraclitan side"[46] implies a Parmenidean division that conjures Emerson as the self-proclaiming emperor of "Being". Though he lived a bourgeois life in Concord thanks to the inheritance from his first wife, earning a living as an orchardist and itinerant lecturer, Emerson was not afraid to make enemies by the publication of his political and metaphysical beliefs that tended to go against the grain. West notes that he tempered his more radical opinions, such as the phrasing of his praise of John Brown, when addressing the academic elite.[47] He probably did this more than once; nonetheless, his restraint was not meant to appease as much as perform a more subtle approach to a dedicated audience. Likewise, West's estimation that "the Emersonian notion of power— the onward transitions and upward crossings achieved by human willpower — celebrates moral transgression at the expense of social revolution" is a mischaracterization.[48] Social revolution was Emerson's principle aim. His support for the sovereignty of native American tribes is well-documented in his speeches and letters of advocacy. His abolitionist stance was passionate, and like his suffragist activism, it began in reluctance and ended in conviction.

Emerson was a scientific dilettante, attending lectures and appropriating terms of science when he could. He was most impressed with John Faraday's lecture about the flow of gasses, which he attended in 1848 in London. Faraday's identification of diamagnetism was seminal in Emerson's imagination.[49] He used the term as a metaphor

---

46   West, American Evasion, 25.

47   Ibid., 23.

48   Ibid., 17.

49   From Emerson's essay "Greatness:" "One fact is clear to me, that diamagnetism is a law of the mind, to the full extent of Faraday's idea; namely, that every mind has a new compass, a new north, a new direction of its own, differencing its genius and aim from every other mind;—as every man, with whatever family resemblances, has a new countenance, new manner, new voice, new thoughts and new character. Whilst he shares with all mankind the gift of reason and the moral sentiment, there is a teaching for him from within which is leading him in a new path, and, the more it is trusted, separates and signalizes him, while it makes him more important and necessary to society. We call this specialty the bias of each individual. And none of us will ever accomplish anything excellent or commanding

to describe the non-conformist tendency of certain characters who, by going against the popular flow, forge new directions. Diamagnetic minds follow their own peculiar bias— "in morals, this is conscience; in intellect, genius; in practice, talent" (W 8:308-09)— and in obeying their bias, they create novel approaches to problems. Emerson defined diamagnetism as "cross-magnetism," (p. 307) or inversed attraction, i.e., repulsion. This aligns with Faraday's conception: a diamagnet is repelled from a magnetic field. Its polarity is flipped, creating a levitating effect.

Emerson's mysticism did not contrast with but substantiated his Heraclitan side. Even as he performs the dialectic in "Nominative and Realist," his "I" is diffused with a generic "we," it seems haphazardly throughout the essay, except at the end where his "I" authorizes the entirety. If Emerson was a dialectician, then he played the Proteus, assuming all of the voices as his own. He contained and dissembled perspectives, spinning them out centrifugally in his considerations. In this sense, his essays are like dances that enact multiple truths.

The dialectical mode is not useful for describing an elusive truth. Indeed, "No sentence will hold the whole truth, and the only way in which we can be just, is by giving ourselves the lie," (p. 246) because the logic of language does not permit contradiction. Emerson wrote that the individual is both partial and universal, but he is also vegetative. At the end of "Nominalist and Realist," the logic of the partialist is juxtaposed against the amusing prospect of the gourd: "We fancy men are individuals; so are pumpkins; but every pumpkin in the field, goes through every point of pumpkin history" (p. 247). His comparison of men to pumpkins mediates the dialectical musings that appear before it. His gnomic wisdom emerges: Emerson's humor communicates where language inevitably fails.

Aye

The enigma of "The Sphinx" is compacted into the multifarious "Aye" at the center of the poem:

---

except when he listens to this whisper which is heard by him alone." (W 7:307)

> Profounder, profounder,
> Man's spirit must dive;
> To his aye-rolling orbit
> No goal will arrive.

Emerson spelled the word that means "yes;" he placed his "aye" in the first half of a hyphenated word, in which it functions as a homonym for "eye," for which the homonym "I" is always available. The orb in the line might be an eyeball, or a circular figure representing life in its basic shape: the earth, the sun, any of the planets. The homonymic associations of the orb include:

1. Eye-rolling, or seeking the heavens to evade monstrous incongruities, dismissal of earthly ironies, incapacity, seizure.
2. Aye-rolling, or wonder, enthusiasm, looking agog.
3. I-rolling, or ecstasy, shifting subjectivity.

In the physical sense, the rolling of the eyes seeks elsewhere, or literally, an interior vision to make sense of jarring perceptions. As an ironic dismissal, eye-rolling responds to stimuli that cannot be interpreted straightforwardly by the senses. It accounts for the need to seek other sources of knowledge beyond the five sense. It seeks meaning outside the apparent, conveying a kind of agony with the present, expressing impatience with the cycle of pride and shame. If the blind bureaucrat rolled his eyes, he might consent to see what he can really do to help you.

Emerson intentionally misspelled "eye" in the context, replacing the organ with the affirmation, colluding the two. His eye-rolling explicitly meant wonder: he wrote in in his journal of his impression of Valletta, Malta, "And though it is very green and juvenile to express wonder, I could not hinder my eyes from rolling continually in their sockets nor my tongue from uttering my pleasure and surprise" (3:30). His "eye" was engrossed by his "aye," suggesting that one should see with the auspicious disposition of the yes-sayer to find what is true beneath the illusions of time. This positive vision acts like the insight of the "intellectual nomad" who seers the film of appearances to discover a unity that connects the I and thou in such a way that subject and object diffuse into one eternal action. The effect lifts a person's gaze from the object to the proper self.

The third instance, "I" rolling, is the most playful and most philosophical hearing of the phrase. Subjectivity is in the domain of the ever-changing code of language. Emerson understood this code as part of the material of the natural world composed in collaboration with human reception. In the dance of meaning between language and the body, shifting subjectivity is the agency of action, wherein impulses defined by spatio-receptivity move the subject whose intention is subdued. Ecstatic becoming is "I-rolling" in the sense that the censorious "I" cedes control so that other aspects of the self, instructed by nature's "benefit," (W 1:205) can be expressed.

Emerson's "I"-rolling, or losing oneself to an action in order to experiment with the possibilities of becoming, is similar to Nietzsche's self-overcoming. The will is dismantled in an exercise of becoming other. Compassion is emphasized. The freedom or fall is *amor fati*: the body's reception determines the direction of becoming so that we can become what we are wont to become in a nature that is greater than ourselves. Nietzsche understood this freedom as a particularly dangerous experiment in *The Gay Science*, in which he entertained the possibility of benevolence as an intrinsic part of nature (p. 375). To cede the will to a natural choreography might look like St. Vitus' dance, a kind of seizure. The problem with Emersonian positivism lay in its assumption that the dancer would promulgate nature's benevolence, rather than effecting destruction. One might become a useful fool, serving political machinations to reinforce religious or nationalistic dogma, operating in the administered morality of "prescribed happiness"[50] in which what is good is understood as an elsewhere. The grace of Emerson's dancer depends not only upon her affinity to nature, what we call her talent, but also on her critical engagement with the here and now.

Moments

Thoreau's abstract interpretation of "The Sphinx" offers an ethos that no one else can supply, considering that these poet-philosophers lived together with similar antisocial inclinations, dedication to reformation, passion for wilderness and disenchantment with

---

50   Adorno, Minima Moralia, 60.

Christian values. In his brief exposition of Emerson's poem, Thoreau, sounding like Nietzsche, wrote, "The naturalist pursues his study with love; while the moralist persecutes his with hate".[51]   The avid curiosity of the naturalist is borne of love, but like Nietzsche, Thoreau disdained the moralist for following dogma and its fear of life.

Like Nietzsche, Thoreau defined love as complicated but thriving: "love is the least moral and the most". Its ambiguity is such that it cannot be grasped by the intellect alone. Conviction occurs in conditions that substantiate our thoughts, which seem to evidence our intuitions by their phenomenal appearance, overriding intellectual apprehension through courage:

> Our bravery is in some moment that we are certain in some degree that our certainty cannot be increased, as when a ray breaks through a gap in a cloud, it darts as far and reaches the earth as surely as the whole sun would have done.[52]

Thoreau suggested that "The Sphinx" was an attempt at describing this moment of conviction, as the mystification of love that occurs in the poem. His description of the conditions of his insight—as a breakthrough that appears in the play of sunlight and clouds—resembles the life-redeeming moment of Nietzsche's *vita femina* (GS 339).

The valuation of moments implies that one has embraced a Dionysian vision of the world. In Stack's interpretation, such moments constitute "an experience, in pathos, of immortality".[53] If chronology projects a false continuity and time actually occurs in discrete moments that can express a compressed eternity, each point of the moment might create a new circle outside of the fatalistic circle. The "full appropriation of the living present" empowers a becoming that precludes shame or guilt, as "we would experience a peace and a height that would take us momentarily, out of the stream of becoming,"[54] as in Emerson's experi-

51   Henry David Thoreau, The Writings of Henry David Thoreau VII, Journal I (1837-1846), 234.

52   Ibid., 235.

53   Stack, Nietzsche & Emerson, 211.

54   Ibid.

ence of the "transparent eyeball" in which he felt himself a channel for "Universal Being" (W 1:10). The imposition of being on becoming is the effect of these peak moments that make suffering worth it: the life that we have is worthy of our complete attention.

Homo Natura

Emerson's project to become a naturalist and Nietzsche's project to bring man back to nature involved the mastery of language in the name of command. Emerson's Poet was charged with the task of affirming the nature of man, affirming logos in the body through the language of whim, and commanding nature through logos. Logos is understood as the natural organism of language, or its metaphorizing power, rather than constructed logic. Nietzsche's task was to master the "spirit," the "something which commands," which desires to "assimilate the new" only insofar as the new adheres to its constitutional growth; what is not useful is ignored (BGE 230). This selective deception is practiced in the process of learning as resistance to the seductions of language. Blind Oedipus and deafened Odysseus are offered as examples: the occlusion of their rationality translates the riddle of nature.

The "terrible basic text homo natura" (231) grounds the learning process, and challenges it with the question: "Why knowledge at all?" Why bother with these distinctions, this sanitation of conscience? Nietzsche proposed that to learn what we are, we must avoid self-flattery. Why do we want to know? We want to change. How can we change? By learning. How do we learn? By assimilation of the strange. What was Nietzsche's estranged truth? To expose the "terrible basic text homo natura" was to confront the Sphinx. Nietzsche's "unteachable" basic text was woman.

Bringing man back to nature, to his powerful state, means to recognize as deceptions the "jingling, festive" (BGE 230) words that signify idealism inherent in conviction. Nietzsche's own conviction was outlined in *Beyond Good and Evil*: his "truths" were wrought in the concept of "woman as such" (230). His problem was woman; his "spiritual fatum" was woman; therefore his resolution of himself had to be through woman, if the purpose was to learn. Learning demands cruelty against oneself, because a man's thirst for knowledge runs "counter to the inclination of his spirit and frequently also to the desires of his heart—by saying No, that is, when he would like to affirm, love, worship" (231). His veiled claim was that he would prefer at heart to be a yes-sayer, to love everything as it ever was, including women.

To "translate man back into nature" (230) means to bring one back to the stability of Greek health, having incorporated the illusion of virtue in the process of learning. The magnanimity of the impulse to interpret the unknown permits a willful ignorance for the sake of a greater knowledge. This hierarchy of organization composes a "will to appearance" (230) that is countered by cultivated circumspection, the honesty that acknowledges bias. In learning, the "fundamental will of the spirit" (213) is a will to power. Falsification occurs in simplifying the complexity of a new experience. One cannot digest the indigestible; it enters the spirit, which Nietzsche likens to a stomach, and is processed or rejected. We pause here to note that Nietzsche took up the metaphor of digestion in *Twilight*, specifically regarding his praise of Emerson, "who instinctively nourishes himself only on ambrosia, leaving behind what is indigestible in things" ("Expeditions" 13). While Nietzsche ruminated on and attempted to digest women, Emerson was not tempted to do the same. For Emerson, the concept of woman was not foreign matter.

The man must be brought back to his homo natura state in order to love; he must understand illusions as such and accept them, as a yes-sayer to the promise of the surface. An appreciation of the veil permits "liberation" by preventing "cruel and merciless attacks" (SE 1). This is the practice of selective ignorance that Odysseus performed with wax in his ears to protect himself from the siren's songs. As Nietzsche willfully deafened himself to the seductions of language, he could not quite close his ears to the Sphinx. His meditation on the value of illusion served as the trajectory from which an abrupt and passionate discourse against female chastity— the fusion of virtue and woman—ensued. While he would have her, he would also not have her: Nietzsche aimed at destroying any version of autonomous woman by claiming that her will to emancipation was merely her will to revenge.

Sacred Savage

We might understand Nietzsche's misogynistic outbursts as an expression of his fear of woman, which as Luce Irigaray has suggested, resembles hydrophobia.[55] In "Heroism," Emerson briefly characterized the classic fear: the "hydrophobia that makes him bark at his wife and babes...indicate[s] a certain ferocity in nature that must have its outlet in human suffering" (p. 249). The rational fear of a fierce nature was extended to the irrational fear of women as symbolized by the Sphinx. Unlike Emerson's poetic Sphinx, who is disarmed in her acceptance of the Poet's love as the answer to her riddle, Nietzsche's duplicitous Sphinx remains a threat. He loves her best when she is dangerous. While he eagerly profaned the ideals of virtue and truth, he would not disrespect the sacred savage.

Nietzsche's scrupulous thinking forced a confrontation with the Sphinx, inciting his attacks, but this occurred when he meant to dissemble idealistic designations, specifically, the female ideal. His attempt to diffuse the sacred fear of woman, to dissemble both woman as monster and woman as eternal feminine, was set up in his revision of *The Gay Science* and in the "Our Virtues" section of *Beyond Good and Evil*, where he describes distinctly female strengths respectively as "artistic" (361) and "natural," (239) combining both of these characteristics in the figure of Baubo, to whom his revision was dedicated. His dedication indicates the reframing of his more earnest ideas in Books I-IV in the mood of parody. As Baubo removed her garments, flashing Demeter in a gesture of comedic consolation, Nietzsche's new Preface and fifth book dressed up his musings in the guise of a hag. Truth is still a woman, but she has become a crone, "who has grounds for not showing her grounds". Life can still be loved, but the quality of this love is shaded by a more skeptical attitude: "It is the love for a woman whom we doubt" (GS P). The impending tragedy at the end of Book IV was thwarted by Nietzsche's humorous, though calculated, self-exposure.

In *The Gay Science.*, there is only one explicit mention of Em-

55   Luce Irigaray, Marine Lover of Friedrich Nietzsche, trans. Gillian Gill (New York: Columbia University Press,1991).

erson, where Nietzsche identifies him as one of the four "masters of prose" (92) of the nineteenth century. In this aphorism, Nietzsche asserts that prose is always in contest with poetry: while poetry's ambitions are serious, prose with poetic pranks intends to be alternately serious and silly. It intends to provoke. Prince Vogelfrei is a trickster: he wants to profane the eternal feminine, to mock his own designs, especially the idealism of the one. Nietzsche's new Preface and added Book V might have had something to do with a desire to make light of "the heaviest weight" introduced at the end of the original book. His revision, composed after he had written *Beyond Good and Evil*, was perhaps meant to profane the threat of the Sphinx.

Dangerous Perhaps

At the end of the second edition of *The Gay Science*, "the question mark" that Nietzsche emphasized implicates "the rendezvous of question and question mark" of the first aphorism of *Beyond Good and Evil* that characterizes the "Beautiful Unity" as "a peculiar, seductive, dangerous ideal". If the Sphinx is suggested at the end of Book V, its terrifying solution might be nothing. Abolishing our "venerations" amounts to nihilism (346). But Emerson's response to the riddle of the Sphinx proclaimed the potential of human creativity: "The Sphinx" from his poem affirmed the right answer in all of the possibles, pointing to humankind's participation in the will to power. His everything provided Nietzsche with a world-affirming principle that acted as the antidote to nihilism.

Nietzsche's allusions to the Sphinx were symbiotic with his vision of a new way of thinking that he called "a philosophy of the dangerous Perhaps," which was dangerous because passion was emphasized over deliberation. Morality was disoriented; common values were easily deranged. One might look at fate straight in the face and grin, not from fear but delight, calling it a "Beautiful Necessity". Nietzsche's point was that only with this sort of silliness can we be serious. His philosophical dance presents an embodied morality that emerged from the axiom of natural benefit, exists outside of language and is as ubiquitous as the "philosophical mysticism"[56] that Lou Von Salomé attributed to him.

Emerson's feminine Sphinx, the one with wings, symbolizes the power that it took to create a new way of seeing nature, giving flight to Nietzsche's damaging female enigma and transforming his Circean Sphinx to the *vita femina*. The "healing effect" that Emerson provided Nietzsche was an anachronistic affirmation of "Being," the *amor fati* of *Ecce Homo*, in which authenticity as the union of appearances and essences was affirmed. In the realm of appearances, where Nietzsche is always upside down, *amor fati* is an acquiescence to the surface, a yes-saying to the illusion of necessity and the necessity of illusion. The ethic presented is that we must dare to try.

---

56   Lou Andrea Von Salomé, Nietzsche, trans. Siegfried Mandel (Champaign, Illinois: University of Illinois Press, 2001), 12.

Part II.

GENIUS

The Seeker

Notes that Nietzsche wrote in his copy of his *Versuche* indicate that the project of Prince Vogelfrei to profane the correctness signaled by the jargon of ideological thinking was provoked by his reading of Emerson. On the cover page of his copy of the book, he wrote:

> Beyond love and hatred, and also of good and evil, a seeker with a clear conscience, cruel to the point of self-torture, un-detected and before all eyes, a tempter who lives by the blood of foreign souls who loves virtue as an experiment, like vice (9:13[21]).

In the context, Nietzsche seems to have cast himself as "the seeker," and Emerson, along with the crowd of historical figures to whom he regularly alludes in his essays, as "foreign souls," though the opposite may also be true. In either case, the image projects a covert masoch-ist with a vampiric appetite for exotica. Nietzsche's strange language aside, we read the rudiment of the Emerson-Nietzsche connection, one that describes an adventurous cosmopolitanism that rejects tradi-tional morality in favor of a more universal, more honest, more aes-thetic, more tentative approach to philosophical, social and psycholog-ical problems. In a word, the correct answer to the Sphinx's question was truth itself, even if it presented as untruth.

Nietzsche's first aphorism in *Beyond Good and Evil* is not a mockery of truth, but a reiteration of the value of the will to truth that he expounded on in "Schopenhauer as Educator". If the apho-rism, "On The Prejudices of the Philosopher," (1) was not a rejection of the will to truth, how are we to interpret the language with which Nietzsche proposed the lie? His irony acknowledges the inability of language to contain abiding truth. His use of Latin to express the force of *amor fati*—the dry seed of his entire philosophy—channels the metaphysics of the dead, which resurrects a pre-Lutheran respect for the arcane. As Ulfers and Cohen observed, Nietzsche held the stance of the Cretan liar: by denying all truth as untrue, he posited truth by the very act of his denial, forcing a direct confrontation with the inadequacy of language to withstand its own logic.[57]   Language at its most precise describes the opposition of values; opposites indicate one another at the baseline of meaning.[58]   Contextual relations create a polarity that incorporates the two. This relational structure suggests that the truth as such is simply the will to meaning-making, charged in the circuit of being.

Nietzsche's contradictions are not semantic actions as much as they are dynamics of thought. One thing once true may not be true again. He resolves the question directly in *The Gay Science*: "'What are man's truths ultimately? Merely his irrefutable errors" (265). This type of thinking describes change, admits possibilities, lacks self-interest, is less predictable and more ambiguous than empirical thinking focused on outcomes. Truth becomes experiment, and like empirical experiment, it must be corroborated.

Altruism and Egoism

Nietzsche's truth, wrought as it was in the ironies of untruth, the seductions of illusion and the outrageous exclamations of his own rhetoric, survived itself in *Ecce Homo* as the will to power, a conduction of the pure pathos of being wherein the truth is superficial. In his autobiography, his conception of appearances is based on the convictions of an altruist that are alternately egoistic. Self-conviction amounts to believing in oneself as a mechanism for believing in everyone else. Truth as an ideal descends to an egoistic apprehension. As Laurence Lampert observed, Nietzsche's "ipsissimosity" (BGE 207) was the mode by which he pointed away from Plato and towards himself, diverging from the general idea as an ontological mode.[59] This move away from the "accursed" self signifies a valuation that is generated through character. Nietzsche's implication of the self, however abject it may be, proposed to empower humankind, thereby improve it ethically.

---

57   Ulfers & Cohen, "Nietzsche's Amor Fati," 13.

58   Ibid.

59   Laurence Lampert, Leo Strauss and Nietzsche (Chicago: The University of Chicago Press, 1996), 26.

The egoist in both Nietzsche and Emerson is always uplifted despite his gravity. Nietzsche's qualification that "he looks 'aloft' unwillingly ….—he knows that he is on a height'—" (265) suggests that a vertiginous state was a condition of his nature Emerson encapsulated this sort of egoistic altruism in his famous phrase from *Nature*:

> Standing on the bare ground, - my head bathed by the blithe air, and uplifted into infinite spaces, - all mean egotism vanishes. I become a transparent eye-ball; I am nothing; I see all; the currents of the Universal Being circulate through me; I am part or parcel of God (10).

In the context, altruism is bound in egotism in two ways. First, in an inverse manner, egotism exits where "Universal Being" begins. Second, more indirectly, Emerson's altruistic detachment occurred in the forest where solitude and a feeling of "perpetual youth" freed his senses. Among the trees, he ceded himself: his complete self-absorption invoked a divine presence that universalized his "I". This is the creation of authenticity, wherein egoism and altruism merge in a moment of spiritual epiphany, making it possible for one to accept the illusion of being as the possession of creative force.

In *Ecce Homo*, where Nietzsche presents himself as an authentic egoist, such self-seduction is magnanimous. The sharp tones of his earlier works flatten into light-hearted self-engagement, exaggerated nearly to the point of caricature. He has small ears, as he wrote in "Why I Write Such Excellent Books," (4) signifying contextually that he is the "anti-ass," the witty agitator of a culture composed mainly of earnest long-ears. He is the negation whose altruistic ego performs as a universalized "I" that acts as subject to the multiplicity. The logic proceeds that If the anti-altruist affirms himself in the complex of fate, he is a boon.

Magnanimity is the prescription in Emerson's "Spiritual Laws": the person who allows herself "the perpetual substitution of being for seeming" is a "benediction," in that she rejects appearances, including her own, and as such, offers "the highest love" (p. 160). Such generosity of spirit is the condition in which feeling replaces seeming. Emerson writes that one should "be a gift" but not give gifts that "shine with borrowed reflection" (p. 160). The social dictates of compliment and apology are dismissed along with other reflexive gestures as "bloated nothingness" (p. 160). He simplifies the point in the essay, "Gifts": "I so admire […] the Buddhist, […] who says, "Do not flatter your benefactors" (W 3:164-5). Walter Kaufmann pointed out that this citation appears nearly verbatim in *The Gay Science* without attribution.[60]

In Nietzsche's reading of "Spiritual Laws," he underlined "Be a gift," and reflected on the idea, possibly, in *Beyond Good and Evil*, where he characterized such greatness of mind: "The noble soul gives as he takes, prompted by the passionate and sensitive instinct of requital, which is at the root of his nature" (265). That Nietzsche found in Emerson a "noble soul" is not disputed, but that his reading of Emerson presented the inspirational gifts of *Beyond Good and Evil* as well as *The Gay Science*, "Schopenhauer As Educator" and *Ecce Homo* is in question here.

Divine Tempter

Nietzsche's solipsistic inclinations were substantiated by his reading of "Spiritual Laws." One wonders whether or not Emerson was his Dionysian philosopher, the "genius of the heart" whom he tempts us to name in "Why I Write Such Excellent Books," (EH 5) where he quotes himself by way of explaining what kind of psychologist he is, citing the passage in *Beyond Good and Evil* in which he first proposed the figure:

> The genius of the heart as is possessed by that great solitary, the divine tempter and born Pied Piper of consciences whose voice knows how to descend into the inmost depths of every soul, who neither utters a word nor casts a glance in which some seduction is not to be found, a part of whose mastery is that he understands the art of seeming—not what he is but that which will bind his followers to press ever more closely upon him, to follow him ever more enthusiastically and whole-heartedly. the divine tempter and born Pied Piper of consciences, whose voice knows how to sink into the inmost

60   Kaufmann, The Gay Science Introduction, 12.

depths of every soul, who neither utters a word nor casts a glance, in which some seductive motive or trick does not lie…. (BGE 295/EH "Books" 5).

Nietzsche coyly forbids us to identify the character, but based on his long descriptions in both books, "the genius of the heart" immediately resembles Emerson, especially considering the triple-play of *Versucher* as tempter, experimenter and essayist.

The image of Emerson as a "born Pied Piper of consciences" is readily available for anyone who has read his essays in which embedded metaphors and allusions glitter like lures attracting universal reflection. Most convincing is the reference to "the art of seeming". The traces of Nietzsche's reading of "Spiritual Laws" emphasize Emerson's relegation of authenticity, an imperative to believe wholeheartedly in the state of mind inclined toward itself in every situation, so that one actually believes what one is saying.

If we examine the context, we see that Emerson is an implied presence in the entire "What is Noble?" section of *Beyond Good and Evil*, in which Nietzsche's "genius of the heart" is first introduced. Nietzsche's natural metaphors pay tribute to Emerson's style as they match his substance. The genius discerns "the pearl of goodness and sweet spirituality, beneath thick black ice, and is a divining rod for every grain of gold, long buried and imprisoned in heaps of mud and sand," (295) with the penetrating vision of Emerson's intellectual nomad, who presides over *The Gay Science* in its original epigraph as "the poet, philosopher and seer" for whom "all things are friendly and sacred, all events profitable, all days holy, all men divine". This is the figure that Nietzsche later recasts as the free spirit.

The series of aphorisms that precede the introduction of the enigmatic Dionysian philosopher construct a context that consistently points to Emerson. The entire section reads like a discussion of ideas that Nietzsche found in Emerson, namely, the claim that the "genius of the heart" does not boast or brag, nor does he seek praise. His ennobled self-conception will suffice. The genius tells us that we are objects for the reflection of divine beauty, meant "to lie placid as a mirror, that the deep heavens may be reflected in them" (295). This is Nietzsche's ambrosial Emerson, whom he eulogizes in *Twilight of The Idols*.

The sectional question, "What is Noble," is answered by an explicit reference to Goethe, (287) who could also have been Nietzsche's "genius of the heart," though the fact that he is named immediately indicates that he is not. While Goethe is identified as the father of reverence, the "genius" is described as the father of enthusiasm, whose likeness to Emerson is directly evoked in the next aphorism:

> One of the subtlest means of deceiving, at least as long as possible, and of successfully representing oneself to be stupider than one really is—which in everyday life is often as desirable as an umbrella—is called enthusiasm, including what belongs to it, for instance, virtue (288).

Enthusiasm was Emerson's principle value, simplified in his famous line from "Circles": "Nothing great was every achieved without enthusiasm" (322). The association of enthusiasm with the appearance of stupidity describes the childish wonder that comes across in Emerson's tones, instantiated by his self-diagnosis of "silliness".[61]

The establishment of enthusiasm as a virtue leads to the declaration that the virtue of "truth" is eternally mutable. Nietzsche identifies the obstacles involved in any attempt at determining a foundational philosophy: behind appearances, there are more appearances (289). This point is emphasized in his marginalia: in his copy of Emerson's "History," he drew three vertical marks next to the phrase, "Under this mask did my Proteus nature hide itself" (6). Though Fabricus' translation was not precise—he translated "Proteus nature" as "natürlicher mensch" or, natural man[62]—Nietzsche got the point: the changeable nature of humankind masks a changing nature, indicating that the surface presents a version of the multifarious face of truth. Truth in appearances is not discredited but framed in temporality, echoing

---

61   Emerson, The Heart of Emerson's Journals, ed. Bliss Perry (London: Houghton Mifflin 1926), 41: "I have so much mixture of silliness in my intellectual frame" (emphasis by Emerson).

62   Digitale Sammlungen der Herzogen Anna Amalia Bibliothek gallery of Nietzsche's copy of Emerson's Versuche, Aus dem Englisch von G. Fabicus: https://haab-digital.klassik-stiftung.de/viewer/image/118058662X/8/OG_0002/

Emerson's claim in "Circles" that "there is no virtue which is final; all are initial," (p. 317) a phrase that Nietzsche underlined heavily.[63] His extension of the point occurs in the same aphorism in which he describes the hermit-philosopher's predicament: in the estimation of truth as foundational, it is understood as shifty. The foundation is unstable, because it is built on an abyss. There is no adequate estimation of truth without acknowledging, as Emerson did, that it is beholden to time's illusions. In other words, truth is available on the surface as an aspect of "the art of seeming".

Art of Seeming

Nietzsche praises his "genius of the heart" not for his authenticity but for his charm, not for what he is but for what he seems to be. That the genius does not profess to be anything more or less than what he seems implies authenticity, but there are no claims made. The privation of the subject appeals: there is simply a voice that knows what to say and how to say it with a knowledge that permits intimacy.

The "art of seeming" is connected with Nietzsche's reading of "Spiritual Laws," where Emerson rebukes those who "accumulate appearances, because the substance is not" (p. 116). The second half of this phrase was underlined by Nietzsche. Emerson's previous sentence, "virtue is the adherence in action to the nature of things and the nature of things makes it prevalent," (p. 116) defines virtue as a condition of nature, rather than as an object of human agency. This thinking is consistent with Nietzsche's logic of indeterminate subjectivity introduced in *Genealogy* 13: the deed is affirmed over the doer, whose consistency with the deed constitutes an integration with nature, which is always the artist in "the art of seeming".

In "Spiritual Laws," Emerson wrote that participation in nature consists of "a perpetual substitution of being for seeming, and with sublime propriety God is described as saying, I AM" (p. 116). By the abrupt conjunction in the middle of the phrase, he connects seeming and being with a divine first-person, and in so doing, confuses man with god. He distances himself from a metaphysical position:

---

63   Ibid.

God's "I AM" is merely "described". Emerson's likening of human essence to divine essence is rhetorical trick meant to connect language to divine power while situating language in the domain of humankind.

Nietzsche was attentive to Emerson's equivocation. On the bottom of this page, he wrote, "I want to rescue men from appearances at every danger. Also no fear of life's approach)" (9:13 [12]). To "rescue men from appearances," means to disabuse them of their customary illusions, in effect to plumb the depths to reveal a truer connection to their own power. The "art of seeming" becomes the conviction of one's being even as being is acknowledged as illusion.

Schein, as Ulfers points out, is an important trope that is related to the dialectics that Nietzsche presented in *The Birth of Tragedy*.[64] Appearance is understood as Apollonian, which is always in tension with Dionysian becoming. Apollonian "seeming" is always all there ever appears to be, but it is also the secondary world. The primary world is Dionysian. It is the position of creation. Through pathos, a "subtraction from appearances,"[65] the Dionysian is revealed as an aesthetic necessity.

The ethic that Nietzsche emphasizes suggests that in order to direct change, we must experience it. This does not mean that we are intentional, rather, it means that we encounter our suffering and become with it, as a part of the process involved in an aesthetic project that is greater than ourselves. The illusion of integrity in the proclamation of "Being" is the condition that elucidates becoming as it occurs. One feels one's way through the worlding world, grounding soundly within it, to become a part of the Dionysian world, which is the true world.

Becoming what one is involves a fashioning of subjectivity. To bring style to one's character challenges one to aestheticize the substance. The first sentence in "Spiritual Laws," "When we look at ourselves in the light of thought, we discover that our life is embosomed in beauty," (p. 131) appeals to the Dionysian sensibility by its reflection on the internal aspect of life. This aspect is the one that counts:

---

64   Ulfers in Friedrich Nietzsche, Dionysian Vision of the World, trans. Ira Allen (Minneapolis: Univocal Press, 2013), p 4.

65   Ibid., 22.

the invisible substance intoxicates the visible. Emerson's emphasis on beauty recognizes external value as well as internal strength, presenting a version of Hegelian aesthetics. This is perhaps how Kaufmann understood Nietzsche's preference for the paintings of Claude Lorrain as connected with his appreciation for Emerson.[66] In the Lorrain paintings that Nietzsche admired, nature appears to be enchanted by the human project, presenting at once a realistic and romantic view.

Nietzsche's "art of seeming" evokes Emerson's "science of appearances," his definition of prudence in the eponymous essay (p. 222). If the risk of the Sphinx is madness, our approach to endless unriddling must be tempered by foresight. Nietzsche's final iteration of *amor fati*, in the *Nachlass* of 1884, names this quality: "Wisdom and love for the wisdom Prolegomena for a philosophy of the future" (11 145). By confusion with Nietzsche's metaphor of wisdom as a woman, *amor fati* becomes the female art of prudence as discretion, not as chastity, about which both Nietzsche and Emerson agreed with the *carpe diem* poets of the Renaissance. Wisdom is always in the service of life. Woman is affirmed along with wisdom.

Lost Philosopher

Points that Emerson makes in "Circles," "Self Reliance," and "Spiritual Laws" were recycled in the "What is Noble" aphorisms that precede the penultimate "genius of the heart" passage in *Beyond Good and Evil*. For example, "every profound thinker is more afraid of being understood than of being misunderstood" (290) invokes both the Emerson of "Self Reliance" ("To be great is to be misunderstood" [p. 392]) and of "Spiritual Laws" ("Nothing seems so easy as to speak and to be understood. Yet a man may come to find that the strongest of defences and of ties,—that he has been understood" [p. 146]). The second example is provocative concerning Nietzsche's reception: if one apprehends that one is actually understood, one must be responsible for oneself. This might account for his fastidious self-styling in *Ecce Homo*.

Emerson's idea that profound thoughts are expressed re-

---

gardless of the will of their thinker invokes a complicity with natural design rather than the designs of the thinker. The idea of owning oneself is riddled with an authority that comes across as temperament. As Nietzsche wrote in his early essay, "Fate and History," "Ask gifted doctors, Emerson says, how much temperament decides, and what, in general, it does not decide?" Indeed, for Emerson, "temperament is final," representing "the chain of physical necessity" (W 3:55). This necessity is propitious: "As the traveler who has lost his way, throws his reins on his horse's neck, and trusts to the instinct of the animal to find his road, so must we do with the divine animal who carries us through this world" (16). Self-trust, which requires good conscience, enables the illusion of agency in a nature determined by benefit.

In "What Is Noble," Nietzsche discusses the invention of the good conscience as a way of simplifying the soul, an Emersonian sensibility that derails intellect in favor of feeling. In the next aphorism, he describes the ideal philosopher as an aesthetic man "who is struck by his own thoughts as if they came from the outside, from above and below, as a species of events and lightning-flashes PECULIAR TO HIM" (292). This description seems to refer to Emerson's "transparent eyeball" epiphany, his experience of ecstatic detachment that revealed the unity behind appearances. The emphasis on peculiarity signifies that aesthetic appreciation cannot be willed. This follows with another description of one who says: "I like that, I take it for my own, and mean to guard and protect it from every one" (293). Emerson shamelessly appropriated, for example, features from Asian religions that he synthesized in his "moral sentiment". The aphorism ends with an invocation to the "*gai sabor*" as a way to protect a person from the sympathy that masquerades as love. The Emerson of "Self Reliance" emphasizes this point; *Beyond Good and Evil* develops it.

Directly preceding the introduction of "the genius of the heart" is "The Olympian Vice," wherein the philosopher and God join in laughter in "an overman-like and new fashion" (294). The philosopher and the god begin their intertwining here and fuse at the end of the next aphorism, where the "genius of the heart" first appears as a Dionysian foreigner, with whom Nietzsche has made connection "mouth to mouth" ("von Mund zu Mund") (BGE 295). We might assume that Nietzsche meant to indicate that "the genius of the heart" was the character whom he connected with his own mouth, who spoke with "the same mouth" (KSA 9:13 [22]), that is, Emerson, his fellow-Sphinx, waging a war against his era from an abyss.

The mouth of the "tempter god" is made to speak: he says that his love for humanity is restricted to those humans who can love—here he alludes to Ariadne —and though he admits that the powers of mankind are prodigious, he claims they might be improved. How? Nietzsche asks. The genius responds, pleasantly, that mankind might become "stronger, more evil, and more profound; also more beautiful-" (295). The explicit promotion of evil might seem uncharacteristic of Emerson, but his implicitly polemical essay, "Compensation," he states quite plainly, "In general, every evil to which we do not succumb is a benefactor" (p. 119). Nietzsche rephrased this in *Twilight of The Idols*: "what does not kill us makes us stronger" ("Maximes and Errors" 8). In order to deconstruct what they understood to be a failing morality, both writers placed ethics in the human realm. According to Emerson, prescribed morality imagined a kind of evil that was "absolute" rather than "privative," like the more sinister sins of greed or dishonesty. To dismantle the absolutism of evil was an attempt to ground and transform it in this world, rather than in the afterlife. As he wrote in "Compensation," "There is one event to good and evil; if I gain any good, I must pay for it; if I lose any good, I gain some other; all actions are indifferent" (p. 120). Nietzsche makes a similar claim in his explicit polemic, *The Genealogy of Morals*: "there is no doer behind the deed" (13).

After the "genius of the heart" blithely repeats his intention to "make humanity stronger, more evil, more profound," as if offering an "enchanting compliment," Nietzsche remarks, "We can see here also that it is not just shame this divinity lacks-" (295) implying that his genius lacks gravitas, the seriousness of the philosopher. This subtle criticism resonates with his explicit criticism of Emerson, written in a letter to Overbeck in 1881:

> I don't know how much I would give to be able to bring it about retroactively, that such a magnificently great nature, so rich in soul and spirit, could have undergone strict discipline,

a really scientific education. As it is, in Emerson we have lost a philosopher.[67]

But we find the lost philosopher as we continue to read. Nietzsche determines that despite his lack of severity, the genius is divine. In fact, the human quality of silliness is what the gods can learn from him. His "daring honesty, truthfulness and love of wisdom" present "the beautifully solemn names of splendor and virtue" (295). As a type of noble savage, he has no need for "venerable rubbish and pageantry," the costume of systemic thought. Nietzsche calls him a god, suggesting that he was referring to "Emerson...one who feeds only on ambrosia," (TI "Expeditions" 13) the nectar of the gods.

We cannot deny that Emerson was a Dionysian philosopher, or anti-philosopher, of whose works Nietzsche had written "I have never felt so at home" (KSA 9:12[68]). As Thomas Brobjer pointed out, Nietzsche's effusive praise of Emerson was not a momentary enthusiasm.[68] Over the course of thirty years, he publicly praised Emerson as "the author richest in thought this century;" (KSA 9:12[151]) "a fantastically great being, rich in soul and spirit;"[69] one of the few "masters of prose" in the nineteenth century (GS 92). He described reading Emerson as uncannily intimate: "I experience Emerson as a twin-soul (Bruder-Seele)," and "Emerson, I have never felt so at home, and in my home, in a book as —I cannot praise it, it stands to me too near" (KSA 9:12[68]). Nietzsche's feeling of extraordinary familiarity with Emerson indicates that perhaps the "genius of the heart" was the writer who was too close to him to name.

Dancing God

The identification of the "genius of the heart" as the symbol of Dionysus is made in both *Ecce Homo* and *Beyond Good and Evil*,

---

67   As cited in Thomas Brobjer, Nietzsche's Philosophical Context: An Intellectual Biography (Chicago: University of Illinois Press, 2008), 25.

68   Ibid.

69   Ibid.

where Nietzsche states plainly that Dionysus is the "ambiguous God". His provocation—his asking us to question the identity of the character—points us to the puzzle of this ambiguity. Some scholars have interpreted the genius as Wagner; others have understood Nietzsche's provocative ambiguity as a rhetorical mechanism for describing the provocative ambiguity of the man-god Dionysus. But to name the genius simply as Dionysus ignores Nietzsche's provocations; it also places a divinely-empowered humanity out of this world, simplifying it in a metaphysical landscape. Humankind's promise in resolving the labyrinth is the correct answer to Nietzsche's puzzle, as long as "the genius of the heart" is meant to represent a mere mortal. Considering Nietzsche's penchant for rhetorical play, the encoding of the genius as nameless and his teasing his readers to discover his true name, signals that the genius is the Dionysian philosopher whom he named "closest to my heart" i.e., Emerson.

In *Twilight*, Nietzsche describes him directly: "Emerson has that gracious and clever cheerfulness which discourages all seriousness; he simply does not know how old he is already and how young he is still going to be" (8). The same phrasing is repeated in Nietzsche's last work, *Will to Power*, regarding the possibility of "new gods":

> So many strange things have passed before me in those time-less moments that fall into one's life as if from the moon, when one no longer has any idea how old one is or how young one will yet be—I should not doubt that there are many kinds of gods— There are some one cannot imagine without a certain halcyon and frivolous quality in their makeup— Perhaps light feet are even an integral part of the concept god— Is it necessary to elaborate that a god prefers to stay beyond everything bourgeois and rational? and, between ourselves, also beyond good and evil? His prospect is *free*—in Goethe's words.— And to call upon the inestimable authority of *Zarathustra* in this instance: *Zarathustra* goes so far as to confess: "I would believe only in a God who could *dance*"— (1038) [Nietzsche's italics].

It is not much of a leap, considering the similarity of Nietzsche's phrasing here to his explicit description of Emerson in *Twilight* that the "halcyon and frivolous makeup" of one who "no longer has any idea of how old one is or how young one will be" in the *Will to Power* was another reference to Emerson, connecting him directly to what Ulfers and Cohen cite as the defining moment of *amor fati*, which occurs in the next paragraph:

> This, my Dionysian world of the eternally self-creating, the eternally self-destroying, this mystery world of the twofold voluptuous delight, my "beyond good and evil," without goal, unless the joy of the circle is itself a goal; without will, unless a ring feels good will toward itself—do you want a name for this world? A solution for all its riddles? A light for you, too, you best-concealed, strongest, most intrepid, most midnightly men?— This world is the *Will to Power*—and nothing besides! And you yourselves are also this *Will to Power*—and nothing besides! (1038) [Nietzsche's italics].

Ulfers and Cohen define *amor fati* as "will to power- and nothing besides," arguing that it is not individuated.[70] In other words, the pathos that infuses nature within and without the subject becomes the determining substrate. In this "mystery world of the two-fold voluptuous delight," there is no solution except the affirmation of its conditions and an orientation to love them, expressed in Dionysian pessimism as the Yes-saying of enthusiasm that makes it possible to become what one is.

Nietzsche as Educator

Stanley Cavell asked what difference it makes to establish a direct lineage between the influenced and the influencer.[71] Does Emerson's influence have a meaningful impact on the content of Nietzsche's philosophy? Nietzsche, through the light of Emerson, is an obstinate character who nonetheless dedicates himself to his readers, especially those with an antinomian tendency for whom he performs riddles,

---

70   Ulfers & Cohen, "Nietzsche's Amor Fati," 13.

71   Stanley Cavell, "Old and New in Nietzsche and Emerson," 231-232.

pithy ambiguities, outrageous monologues, neologisms— all those expressions that reach the reader outside of language. We are familiar with his resistance to being read. In *Ecce Homo*, where he provides a key to his interpretation by referring to his earlier essay "Schopenhauer as Educator," which he says contains his "most secret history," ("Thoughts" 3) he wrote: "I am one, my writings another" ("Books" 1). The one that he professed to be at the moment was mostly harmless, but he wrote later, "I am not a man, I am dynamite," and just after that, "Maybe I am a clown" ("Fatality" 1). Which are we to read, his mood or his word? If we take him at his word, understanding that his word was wrought in a scheme of reference and self-reference, he does not exactly mean what he is saying but it seems that he means what he says at last when he calls himself "Nietzsche as Educator" ("Thoughts" 3). His contradictions were meant to instruct.

Nietzsche, who conjured future readers as oppositional as he was, composed a riddled dialogue whose pedagogical concern is plain: the encoding of Emerson as the "genius" was his redemption of benevolence. As he wrote in a letter to his good friend, Overbeck:

> Emerson, with his Essays, has been a good friend and someone who has cheered me up even in dark times; he possesses so much *scepsis*, so many 'possibilities' that with him even virtue becomes spiritual.[72]

We know that Nietzsche connected his revaluation of virtue with Emerson because he wrote the title of his book, *Beyond Good and Evil*, on the end page of his copy of the *Versuche*. His estimation of virtue was polemical; he valued virtue as much as he valued truth, that is, virtue in evil, or truth in untruth, or whatever is *Beyond Good and Evil*. In a broad way, Emerson's writing promoted an ethics situated outside of traditional Christian morality, specifically in the assertion of "Being" as a metaphysics of presence.

As long as Emerson is cloaked as the "genius of the heart," "Being" persists as metaphysics in disguise. The disguise is needed because "virtue" must be protected from the language that grasps, like

---

72   As cited in Brobjer, Nietzsche's Philosophical Context, 25.

Cavell's "unhandsome" hand.[73] Nietzsche's *tricherie salutaire* activates a Dionysian force to subvert the Apollonian surface. In other words, his secrecy was the way to freedom in an attempt to forge a new philosophy that risked nonsense. To affirm the difference between philosophy and literature means to affirm the intellect and emotions, the deliberation and the impulse, the theory and the thing itself. Conditioning these differences, in Emerson's thinking, is feasible to the "most impressionable brain," which "yields to a current so feeble as can be felt only by a needle delicately poised" (W 6:45). In other words, will or intellect alone cannot unleash being. Unlike Hindu karma, which is bound in the deed, Emerson's "Being" is unbound in action, and thought is action. Intentionality is apprehended in the immanence of history.

Mighty Heritage

Cavell's question regarding whether American's evasion of philosophy is an evasion of justice is answered in "Spiritual Laws:" in a word. Patience, taking into account that patience means suffering. But it is only through the animal of language—Nietzsche's words that bleed—that the dynamics of fate and freedom begin their play. The question that Cavell returns to is: how can philosophy look like Emerson's writing?[74] His language, it seems, is always going on holiday. Dancing prose invites a correspondence among terms of nature into a logic that determines. The "irresistible dictation" of "Fate" must be willfully counteracted by its "condition," which, as Cavell emphasized, means living language, or communication, as in saying with (p. 4).[75] Emerson's affirmation of both fate and freewill indicates that we must compose our own "condition" in the development of an integrity that acts like a muscle: "There can be no driving force except through the conversion of the man into his will, making him the will, and the will

---

73   Cavell, "Finding as Founding," 117.

74   Cavell, "Aversive Thinking: Emersonian Representations in Heidegger and Nietzsche," 142-3.

75   Cavell, "Emerson, Coleridge, Kant," 71.

him" (p. 30). The will to power as resistance to "irresistible dictation" executes an ethic of "fate against fate," (p. 26) in which a person as "a part of fate" (p. 22) performs her destiny with a will to direct it. Somewhere between dictation and reception, laws are proposed.

Cavell was concerned with Emerson's position as a thinker "not up to the pitch of reason" of the European philosophical tradition.[76] But if we understand Nietzsche's work as the processing of Emerson's, and Nietzsche's writing as germinal in the development of continental philosophy, having influenced nearly every philosopher who came after him, then we must take Emerson as a forebear of continental philosophy.

In American philosophy, Emerson's heir apparent was William James. But James was a sober thinker. His writing lacks Emerson's heat. James Baldwin, it seems, was closest to him.[77] The passion, skepticism and elegance of both Baldwin's and Emerson's writings express a fierce and loving vision. Indeed no other essayists have apprehended the culture with such spirited criticism of the American project. Unlike Emerson, who enjoyed the privileges of wealth and whiteness, Baldwin, a black man, wrote from a palpably tragic worldview. These final passages of his essay, "Nothing Personal," describe the meaning of the *amor fati*:

> It is a mighty heritage, it is the human heritage, and it is all there is to trust. And I learned this through descending, as it were, into the eyes of my father and my mother. I wondered, when I was little, how they bore it-for I knew that they had much to bear. It had not yet occurred to me that I also would have much to bear; but they knew it, and the unimaginable rigors of their journey helped them to prepare me for mine. This is why one must say Yes to life and embrace it wherever it is found-and it is found in terrible places; nevertheless, there it is; and if the father can say, Yes. Lord. the child can

---

76   Cavell, "Finding as Founding," 120.

77   Both Cornel West and Eddie S. Glaude, Jr. have identified Baldwin as Emerson's heir: West, 2004 and Glaude, August, 2020. West, Cornel. 2004. Democracy Matters: Winning the Fight against Imperialism. New York: Penguin Press

learn that most difficult of words, Amen. For nothing is fixed, forever and forever and forever, it is not fixed; the earth is always shifting, the light is always changing, the sea does not cease to grind down rock. Generations do not cease to be born, and we are responsible to them because we are the only witnesses they have. The sea rises, the light fails, lovers cling to each other, and children cling to us. The moment we cease to hold each other, the moment we break faith with one another, the sea engulfs us and the light goes out.[78]

This notion of a descent into the eyes of history—those eyes bound to us by the familiar complexity of love and suffering—affirms the love and suffering in our immediate lives. Acquiescence to such strife confirms a loving-with our conditions, and a loving-with one another, conjuring the prospect of an indeterminate future that is as tenuous as our embrace.

Naive and True

Reading Emerson through Nietzsche's eyes focuses on principles that are impersonal but universal. For Nietzsche, Emerson was not the sage of Concord, but of a nature of cosmopolitans connected to one another "beyond everything bourgeois and rational" (WP 1038). Emerson describes the universal mind, the principle behind the metaphysical structure that he calls the Oversoul, in this passage from "Compensation":

> The heart and soul of all men being one, this bitterness of His and Mine ceases. His is mine. I am my brother and my brother is me. If I feel overshadowed and outdone by great neighbors, I can yet love; I can still receive; and he that loveth maketh his own the grandeur he loves. Thereby I make the discovery that my brother is my guardian, acting for me with the friendliest

---

78   James Baldwin, "Nothing Personal," Contributions in Black Studies: Vol. 6 , Article 5, 2008.

designs, and the estate I so admired and envied is my own. It is the nature of the soul to appropriate all things. Jesus and Shakespeare are fragments of the soul, and by love I conquer and incorporate them in my own conscious domain (124).

Alongside this passage in his *Versuche*, Nietzsche wrote two words: "naive and true".[79] This response contrasts with his rejection of "History"'s "universal mind," next to which Nietzsche had written "Nein! Aber es ist ein Ideal!"[80] It is precisely such idealism that Nietzsche would reject, but through his consideration of Emerson's intellectual nomad, the philosophical father of his own "free spirit," he accepted the possibility of the kind of benevolence associated with universal love that issues from the eye of the beholder.

In the "Wherewith we see the ideal" section of *Human, All Too Human*, Nietzsche describes the mechanics of this axiomatic vision: the "virtue" that prevents a person from reaching "an intellectual or moral freedom" is "efficiency" (86). Clearly, he meant to disparage such virtuosity, as he meant to praise the "imperfection" and other "shortcomings" (86) that enable one to create from a position of moral responsibility. This visual glossing was associated with his idealism of subjectivity.

Connected to "History," it is also an aspect of the universal mind. The essay begins with a poem ending in these lines:

> I am owner of the sphere,
> Of the seven stars and the solar year,
> Of Caesar's hand, and Plato's brain,
> Of Lord Christ's heart, and Shakespeare's strain (2).

The poem echoes "Compensation," where Emerson makes the same

---

79   Nietzsche's short responses to Emerson's essays—his more emotional and less substantial marginalia—have been indexed in an online appendix created by the Oxford University Press to accompany the recently published book by Benedetta Zavatta, Individuality and Beyond: Nietzsche Reads Emerson (London: Oxford University Press, 2019): https://global.oup.com/us/companion.websites/9780190929213/ap/

80   Ibid.

points about the incorporation of the universal mind, involving the same characters. Nietzsche's response to it was written in the margins next to the poem:

> O our greed! I feel nothing of selflessness, but a self-seeking self, which sees through many individuals, as through his eyes, and grasps with his hands, a self which also recaptures the whole past, which does not want to lose anything that might belong to him at all (9: 13 [7]).

The image that Nietzsche evokes resembles his 100 eyed Argus, who appears in *Human All Too Human* as a form of "his Io- I mean his ego" (223). The self -seeking of this mythological character, feminized by the accidental "Io," leads to "universal knowledge" and "universal direction" (223). That these marginalia were recycled verbatim in *The Gay Science* as "The sigh of one who comes to know" (249) suggests that he had digested Emerson's universal mind, with some cautionary repulsion. Nietzsche's reckoning with Emersonian universalism in his most deliberate project indicates a reconstitution of his theoretical framework.

Benedetta Zavatta has claimed that the two philosophies are fundamentally different. She casts Emerson in a Calvinist mold, and Nietzsche as a psychologist of the abstract,[81] taking his "naive and true" marginalia as a psychological operation concealed "beneath a mask of a sort of universal love and mystical union of all beings". It seems more likely that he was responding earnestly to the metaphysics of the surface. In his reading of Emerson, Nietzsche wore no mask: *amor fati* is "universal love and mystical union of all beings". A fundamental distinction between the two writers is that Emerson's essays were often first lectures, while Nietzsche's performed purely as text.

That one incorporated the other into a mythological idealism through the abridgement of language intensifies their emotional dynamics. Nietzsche's affirmation of Emerson encodes pathos at its most acute, dignifying the suffering of the young. He was perhaps

---

81   Benedetta Zavatta, "Historical Sense as Vice and Virtue in Nietzsche's Reading of Emerson," Journal of Nietzsche Studies, Vol. 44, No. 3 (Philadelphia: Penn State University Press, 2008), 22, note 53.

the only reader of Emerson who understood the dynamics of whim, interpreting it as an ethic of experimentalism. Time and the self are eradicated in an ethic that qualifies thought as action. This looks like a physics of the soul, rather than a relinquishment to metaphysics.

Alienated Majesty

Nietzsche wrote these lines from Emerson's "Self Reliance" in his copy-book:

> In every work of genius we recognize our own rejected thoughts: they come back to us with a certain alienated majesty (9:17[21]).

It seems that he recognized his "own rejected thoughts" in Emerson, and they came back to him in a way that is best described by looking at another of his notes, written on the back cover of his *Versuche*:

> Be a plate of gold, things will be written on you in golden letters" (9:13[6]).

The note alludes to Exodus 28:36, "Make a plate of pure gold and engrave on it as on a seal: holy to the Lord". Nietzsche substituted "make a plate of gold" with "be a plate of gold," inferring that one is to become the object, rather than acquire it. His phrasing recalls Emerson's nominalization of the predicate: one should not become virtuous, but be virtue; one should not become intelligent, but be intelligence. This illusion of subjectivity—the superabundant condition of "The Great Health" (GS 382)—empowers a language that is inspirited in the character who can bear it, the one who can withstand the stamp of universal meaning. "Ipsissimosity" dissolves into the realm of Hindu spirituality, in which *I am that* is the moniker for omnipotent being. Beyond the system of Hinduism, which neither Nietzsche nor Emerson privileged, "Being" remains ambiguous.

The note elucidates the importance of Heraclitus as a mediator between Emerson and Nietzsche. The cryptic form of the saying, the passive position associated with humility, the ubiquitous instruction of pathos and the importance of substance available in appearance are Heraclitan interpretations wherein absolutes are discernable by their absence.

Part III.

ARIADNE

The Riddle of Ariadne

The quiet but persistent metaphor of Ariadne is epigraphical to the complex love of the "genius of the heart," which became, in Nietzsche's reading, the story of *amor fati*. Emerson as the "genius of the heart" acted as Ariadne, guiding Nietzsche through the labyrinth where he found himself as the Sphinx, puzzling through indirections, dissolved in another abyss. Metaphor appears as trace, like the outlines of a fossil on successive layers, functioning as an indication of philosophical "truth". The hermeneutical aspect is indeed the only truth. The Ariadne-Dionysus complementarity that Deleuze discerned[82] in Nietzsche's writing envisions the antithetical in an essential opposition that operates as what Ulfers and Cohen call "chiasmic unity".[83] This was also Emerson's resolution of the riddle of the Sphinx. The way out of the labyrinth is neither left nor right, but both: at the axis of opposition is the circle of fate. Ariadne's thread leads back to itself. In the myth, the ultimate becoming is represented by the Minotaur, slain by Theseus with the provided weapon. The weapon that Emerson provided Nietzsche, the word that became sword, was "Being," precisely as the performance of becoming in the framework of the labyrinth as a metaphor for fate. The acceptance of such pretension requires a kind of faith that acts linguistically like Ariadne's thread.

For both Nietzsche and Emerson, Ariadne represented the *Corona borealis*, woman constellated in the night sky. The eloquent passion of her disprized love and her act of heroism in rescuing Theseus from the Minotaur elevated her in Nietzsche's esteem above even Athena, who was respected but never human enough—she never suffered enough—to earn the kind of position that Ariadne took in Nietzsche's female pantheon. Ariadne is wickedly clever. She has a trained ear attuned to the sorcery of the natural world, but her chief strength is the kind of critical thinking that empowers *techne* in the forms of her

82   Gilles Deleuze, Nietzsche and Philosophy, trans. Hugh Tomlinson (New York, Columbia University Press,1983):13.

83   Ulfers and Cohen, "Amor Fati," 4

thread and sword. The northern constellation crowns the majesty of human reason; it directs most divinely by its visibility in the night sky, not by its whisperings, murmurings, or songs As a woman of action, she knows how to slay the Minotaur and can find her way out of the labyrinth, but for Nietzsche, her most heroic quality was her willingness to love in spite of loss.

Ariadne's first riddle was the labyrinth, a symbol of fate. Her solution—the prowess of her thread and sword that enabled the human to "find the right path even in every labyrinth" (BGE 295)—was only available to the beloved, indicating the continuous relation between knowing and feeling. Ariadne's second riddle was love. This double riddle becomes a triple riddle In "the genius of the heart" sections, where Nietzsche tempts his readers to guess the identity of his genius by forbidding it, so that only those willing to defy him can discover its meaning. Attached to Ariadne, the meaning of the genius is *amor fati*: double-affirmation, or the willingness to suspend disbelief in the illusion of being.

The "genius of the heart" section in *Beyond Good and Evil* presents Ariadne as a model of courage and cleverness in the one human being that Nietzsche could love. She appears abruptly near the end of the section, the part that is not recycled in *Ecce Homo*, in an allusion the genius makes to her:

> He said it this way once, "In some circumstances, I love human beings" - and in saying that, he was alluding to Ariadne, who was present - "for me a human being is a pleasant, brave, inventive animal which has no equal on earth; it finds the right path even in every labyrinth..." (p. 295).

That Nietzsche would allude to an allusion is characteristic of his cryptic style, one that seems to cloak the identity of the goddess in a triple-riddle connected with Emerson.

Clearly, If Emerson was the "genius of the heart," he must have made a reference somewhere in his work to Ariadne, specifically in the first series of essays that Fabricus translated and Nietzsche read. In all of Emerson's works, he alludes to Ariadne only once, in the essay, "Heroism," which was published in the *Versuche* and marked by Nietzsche's notes. The allusion appears near the beginning of the essay in an epigraphical excerpt from John Fletcher's play, "The Triumph of Honor":[84]

> Sophocles. No, I will take no leave.
> My Dorigen, Yonder, above, 'bout Ariadne's crown,
> My spirit shall hover for thee (p. 246).

The lines describe the moment in the play before Sophocles' impending execution, when his beloved Dorigen enters armed with a sword, defiant in her will to die with him. Her willingness to sacrifice herself for Sophocles is the triumph that delivers both from execution. Like Ariadne, Dorigen is a warrior and protectress who serves none but her beloved.

Sophocles' response to Dorigen, "To die is to begin to live," is the rudiment of Emersonian *amor fati*, developed in "Heroism" towards the affirmation of "inextinguishable being" (p. 264). Emerson's reasoning runs as follows: because man "is born into the state of war," (p. 249) heroism always requires an antinomian impulse in the struggle against falsehood. Heroes "play their own game in innocent defiance of the Blue-Laws of the world" (p. 256). Virtue is "a shade" (p. 255). The "transcendent properties" belong to those who domesticate "the Greek energy, the Roman Pride" (p. 257). A "stoicism of the blood" (248) and dissociation from loveless hoards will protect the hero from violence against his character when his opinions are denounced as "incendiary" (p. 263). The hero should always "die when it is not better to live" (p. 262). This affirmation of death is doubled by Dorigen's promise, which "made death impossible," resolving being as "absolute" (p. 264).

The initial epigraph in the essay is a quote from Mohammed regarding the omnipresence of war, after which appears Emerson's poem describing the hero's Promethean struggles. One might consider the dramalogue featuring Dorigen that appears after the first two as a third epigraph, as its meaning is rephrased in the end of the essay where Emerson returns to the notion of immortal love described in the play. The last two sentences are particularly germane to Nietzsche's reading regarding the configuration of *amor fati*:

---

84   John Fletcher & Nathan Field, Four Plays in One (London: Copyright Group Limited, 2018).

And yet the love that will be annihilated sooner than treacherous has already made death impossible, and affirms itself no
mortal but a native of the deeps of absolute and inextinguishable being (p. 264).

Nietzsche circled these lines, underlined them, and placed two question marks in the margins alongside. We note that his question marks
seem to be more emphatic than his exclamation points. He also rarely
circled the text he read, indicating that the lines were extraordinarily
meaningful to him.

What was the meaning of these lines to Nietzsche? In the
context of "Heroism," the "love that will be annihilated sooner than
treacherous" is a reference to Dorigen, who volunteers to die alongside Sophocles. Dorigen's willingness aligns her "as a native to the
depths of absolute and inextinguishable being" (p. 264). The effect of
her affirmation institutes a new circle of meaning that is the same as
Ariadne's: *amor fati*, the love whose passion constitutes "Being."

Fair Girl

Of all of Emerson's essays, "Heroism" is the most Nietzschean in timbre: it is somewhat rude, starting from its formal double-epi-
graph, the second of which features the lines: "The hero is not fed on
sweets/Daily his own heart he eats" (p. 244). Nietzsche's annotations
of the essay indicate his attention to its themes of war and contempt.
These lines in particular describe a kind of contempt that is unchar-
teristic of Emerson:

There seems to be no interval between greatness and meanness. When the spirit is not master of the world, then it is its
dupe. Yet the little man takes the great hoax so innocently,
works in it so headlong and believing, is born red, and dies
gray, arranging his toilet, attending on his own health, laying
traps for sweet food and strong wine, setting his heart on a
horse or a rifle, made happy with a little gossip or a little praise,
that the great soul cannot choose but laugh at such earnest
nonsense (p. 252).

One can imagine Emerson's voice here as appealing directly to Nietzsche, especially regarding the need for "mastery" and disdain for petty valuations. Though the lines resonate "meanness," the quality of Emerson's criticism is sweetened by his acquittal of "the little man" who "takes the great hoax so innocently" (p. 252). Emerson does not accuse "the little man" but mocks him good naturedly; thus did his well-tempered contempt appeal to the little men themselves.

In Nietzsche's reading of "Heroism," this passage was marked by a single vertical line in the margin,[85] indicating his attention to the theme of contempt. His similar annotations, single vertical lines, surround passages regarding war, self-trust, the dignity of the spirit, and the problem of sympathy, all of which are typical Emersonian themes. Nietzsche's most emphatic marks—double, or triple vertical lines, question marks and circling of text—occur aside lines signifying themes of magnanimity, virtue, defiance, the approach of the heroine, and the discernment of a universal but aristocratic code of love. These ideas circulate throughout Emerson's works, with the notable exception of the heroine's appearance.

At the center of this essay, though still at sea, floats "the fair girl" (p. 259). Like Ariadne, she occupies a liminal space between the earth and sky. She hovers on the horizon of the actual like Dorigen. The section starts with a description of potential heroes: young, male, blustering idealists whose revolutionary contempt only makes them ridiculous when they shrink before the actual as if "their heart fainted" (p. 259). These heroes are cast aside by the unceremonious appearance of the heroine. The young men fail, and-

> What then? The lesson they gave in their first aspirations is yet true; and a better valor and a purer truth shall one day organize their belief. Or why should a woman liken herself to any historical woman, and think, because Sappho, or Sévigné, or

---

85   Nietzsche's short responses to Emerson's essays—his more emotional and less substantial marginalia—have been indexed in an online appendix created by the Oxford University Press to accompany the recently published book by Benedetta Zavatta, Individuality and Beyond: Nietzsche Reads Emerson (London: Oxford University Press, 2019): https://global.oup.com/us/companion.websites/9780190929213/ap/.

De Staël, or the cloistered souls who have had genius and cultivation do not satisfy the imagination and the serene Themis,
none can,—certainly not she? Why not? (p. 259)

First we notice the abrupt way that Emerson introduces the female
—with a casual conjunction, the rhetorical "Or" that tricks the reader into imagining the approach of the Apollonian woman. "Why
not?" Emerson rather magnanimously asks, presenting his offering of
the coming heroine, and in this spirit, we take up his consideration.

Certainly, Nietzsche took it up, as is clear by the bold double
vertical lines he marked next to the paragraph's last two sentences:

The silent heart encourages her; O friend, never strike sail to a
fear! Come into port greatly, or sail with God the seas. Not in
vain you live, for every passing eye is cheered and refined by
the vision (p. 259).

The strengths of this "fair girl" are her "happiest nature," her will-
fulness, detachment, curiosity and self-trust, all of which reveal "the
power and the charm of her newborn being" (p. 259). She "repels
interference," indicating that the antinomian tendency is natural to her.
Perhaps she will arrive, perhaps she will stay at sea; Emerson's encour-
agement applies either way. As the object of his vision, she is a muse, a
prospect and an inspiration, located between history and imagination.
The actual heroine is called upon; in the meantime, her mythical appearance on the horizon will suffice.

Emerson's featuring of women of action in "Heroism" was
exceptional: he did not privilege the female gender in his other works,
although the sexual identities of male and female that occur in the
natural sciences informed his view of the ideal character, composed of
both genders.[86] His mystical principle of "Being" was also gendered:
"the Godhead" that he described in the fifth book of his journal encompasses "the Male and Female principle in nature" (p. 337). Regard-

---

86   "A highly endowed man with a good intellect and good conscience is a
man woman" and "hermaphrodite is then the symbol of the finished soul." As
quoted in Richardson: Robert D. Richardson, Jr, Emerson: Mind on Fire (Berkley
& Los Angeles: The University of California Press): 383.

less of whether one is in fact a man or a woman, one can access the other gender through imaginative internalization of the distinguishing qualities. Cultivating the female nature in himself by accepting the friendship of women was one of the ways that Emerson opened himself to possibilities that gender supplied. These possibilities became potentialities in "Heroism". The heroine's inauguration coincided with the presence of Ariadne, whose thematic aspect presented the power of the female.

Littoral Women

Whereas in most of Nietzsche's writings, the female, as Derrida elegantly wrote, "is coiled within the labyrinth of the ear,"[87] she is visible in *The Gay Science*, specifically in "Women and their action at a distance," which begins "Do I still have ears? Am I all ear and nothing else?" (60). Nietzsche's secrets are always signaled by a perking of the ears. His secret here is the presence of Emerson, who appears barely disguised as "the noble enthusiast":

> Yet! Yet! My noble enthusiast, even on the most beautiful sailing ship there is so much sound and noise, and unfortunately so much small, petty noise! The magic and the most powerful effect of women is, to speak the language of the philosophers, action at a distance, actio in distans: but that requires, first and foremost - distance! (60)

By the grammar of Nietzsche's sentence, it appears as if Emerson is intentionally invoked, specifically regarding his consideration of the littoral female in "Heroism". A preceding aphorism sets up the reference: in "The Ultimate Noble-mindedness," Nietzsche defines the noble mind as passionate, humble, courageous, uncommon and antinomian, embodying "a self-sufficiency that overflows and communicates to men and things" (55). Emerson as an exemplar of "What is Noble" is presented indirectly in *Beyond Good and Evil*, but in *The Gay Science*, Nietzsche seemed to speak directly to him, addressing him in the vocative.

---

87   Derrida, Spurs, 43.

At the beginning of GS 60, we understand that what Nietzsche hears is the roaring of the ocean; what he sees is a "large sailing ship," appearing on the horizon like a Fata morgana, imposing an orchestral silence upon him that transforms him into a "spirit-like, silent, watching, gliding, hovering intermediate being," like the ship itself, so that he imagines he is the ship, gliding along, touched by strange magic (60). He associates this unworldly vision with women, whose qualities of "happiness and seclusion" echo the description of Emerson's heroine:

> When a man stands in the midst of his own noise, in the midst of his own surf of projects and plans, he is also likely to see gliding past him silent, magical creatures whose happiness and seclusion he yearns for - women. He almost believes that his better self lives there amongst the women: in these quiet regions even the loudest surf turns into deathly silence and life itself into a dream about life (60).

As the symbol of Nietzsche's anima, these women represent "his better self," but because "his own noise" is too distracting, and "all great noise makes us place happiness in silence and distance," they have to remain at sea (60).

One could say that Nietzsche's qualification of Emerson's "fair girl" extended from his customary rejection of idealism, but he seems to accept the idealism of "Women... at a distance" as long as they are far away. The terrifying specters that seem to invade his conscience in *Beyond Good and Evil* and *Ecce Homo* appear in *The Gay Science* as dreamy beings that appeal only via the pathos of distance, acting as the remote form of his "woman as such". The old women of a subsequent aphorism, who "believe the superficiality of existence to be its essence" affirm the happiness of the maritime women who seem to "move over existence," but their skepticism damages Nietzsche's dream by disclaiming its "virtue and depth" as "the very desirable veil over a pudendum" (64). His romantic vision is debased by its attachment to anatomy, and replaced later with "artistic distance" that allows "freedom over things" (107).

The silencing of Nietzsche's ever-present internal feminine indicates an inclination to disdain the female part of his character. Del Caro proposed that "Nietzsche's anima, to use Jung's term, is very much alive throughout *Zarathustra* in the figure of the disguised Ariadne," observing that in the process of writing, Nietzsche "felt compelled to practice this seductive, disguised, ironic (masked) suppression of the feminine".[88]   As he pointed out, *Zarathustra* embraces the female aspect in his one wife, the woman who represents eternity.[89]

Ariadne-Eternity

The Ariadne-eternity complex begs the question: how does eternal recurrence correspond to the female figure? Nietzsche's valuation of Ariadne as the beloved who has suffered but still affirms love indicates that the great weight of eternal recurrence is bearable only because the *vita femina* is worth enduring. This connection is explicit in *Ecce Homo*, "Why I Write Such Excellent Books":

> Such things have never been written, never been felt, never been suffered: only a God, only Dionysus suffers in this way. The reply to such a dithyramb on the sun's solitude in light would be Ariadne. ... Who knows, but I, who Ariadne is! To all such riddles no one heretofore had ever found an answer; I doubt even whether any one had ever seen a riddle here. One day *Zarathustra* severely determines his life-task—and it is also mine. Let no one misunderstand its meaning. It's a yea-saying to the point of justifying, to the point of redeeming even all that is past (8).

The description of the "sun's solitude in light" that "would be Ariadne" places her as the personification of *vita femina*, wherein clouds part to reveal the sunlit moment that redeems all moments. Ariadne reverses the catastrophe of Nietzsche's being and becomes the emblem of *amor fati* by way of this justification. That Ariadne is a riddle is consistent

---

88   Adrian Del Caro, review of Paul Bishop, The Dionysian Self: C. G. Jung's Reception of Friedrich Nietzsche, in The Journal of Nietzsche Studies (Berlin and New York: Walter de Gruyter,1995).

89   Del Caro, Nietzsche Contra Nietzsche: Creativity and The Anti-Romantic (Baton Rouge and London: Louisiana State University Press, 1989): 169.

with Nietzsche's rhetoric: she will remain arcane. She is not read, nor will be read. This is the psychology of the eternal feminine.

The Dionysian space is unfathomable, except through Ariadne who holds its secrets. In Nietzsche's poem "Ariadne's Lament," the voice of Dionysius assures her, "You have my ears," instructing her to "put a clever word in them". Deleuze understood that the clever word was Yes, an affirmation of "the loving feminine power" bestowed by the lover who can affirm twice, first as mere positivity and second, as the possessed, the complement of Dionysius that symbolizes the constitution of being and becoming.[90] The double-riddle of Ariadne is presented by Dionysus: "I am your labyrinth". Her challenge becomes self-overcoming through the other, even if the other is a version of the self:

> Hunted by you, Thought!
> Nameless! Cloaked! Horrid!
> You hunter behind clouds!
> Struck down by your lightning,
> Your scornful eye, glaring at me out of the dark!

The identification of Dionysus with Ariadne contrives the Dionysus-Ariadne complementarity, yet the two figures are clearly singular. The other is first identified as "Thought," and later as "the unknown god," revealed as Dionysus. If "Thought" is her tormentor, her struggle is internal; if Dionysus is her tormenter, her struggle is with another. In either case— both are suggested— Ariadne sees herself "like a dog" who wallows before the "Thought" or the god that wishes to possess her. Though her pride resists, she ultimately submits, having endured an education in self-hatred by way of humiliation. Dionysus asks, "Must one not first learn to hate oneself in order to love oneself?" suggesting that the knowledge that results from her education is self-love through affirmation of the other, even if the other is her love-besotted self.

In "Ariadne's Lament," she is redeemed by her "ultimate happiness" in union with the other that reappears in the poem in the form of a lightning bolt, i.e., Dionysus, who seems to have stolen the tool

90   Deleuze, Nietzsche and Philosophy,187.

of Zeus. This association with Giambattista Vico's first word, Pa—the sound of a thunderbolt—does not go unnoticed, considering that language is the Dionysian prescription. "The clever word" that Ariadne is meant to affirm proclaimed a questionable authority.

Contradiction of Amor fati

The question of *amor fati* has always been how to reconcile fate and free will. The negotiation between fate and freewill for both Emerson and Nietzsche acknowledges unity as a multiplicity that presents the illusion of creative subjectivity. The "Blessed Unity" is the effect of becoming oneself through the other; in this sense it is not strictly unity. In Emerson's thinking, the illusion of subjectivity comes across in the subject's assent to whim, an imaginative reception that demands a playful becoming rather than a plotted becoming. Assenting to whim is the subject's permission to become other to herself in a moment of grace, acting upon the benevolence that operates in nature. Affective thought corresponds to the material of the universe that Nietzsche identifies as pathos, inspiring sensationalized subjectivity in action that flows in a propitious direction, in effect merging the dancer with the dance. Thought should be like a dance, Nietzsche wrote, one that performs the world's antithetical principles. The dancer guides pathos by becoming with it.

How does one choreograph thought If subjectivity is null? The illusion of subjectivity is directed by declaration—a clever word —reception to which is only available to one who has "good ears," like Ariadne, or one who can be instructed. For Emerson, the moment that one becomes "a lover of uncontained and immortal beauty" (W 1:10) engages one in the multiplicity of nature. To engage propitiously in this multiplicity—to act as a "piece of fate"—requires an education. In other words, it is not quite impulsive but trained by the thought that interacts in nature regarding what is auspicious.

Emerson's conception of the interconnection between the human and nature that is expressed through whim begets the thought of "the universal mind," (W 1:3) with which humankind interacts in key moments when the real and representational collude. But the "Blessed Unity" remains two. In his long journal entry of May 26, 1837, in an attempt to describe the individual, Emerson wrote:

> A believer of Unity, a seer of Unity, I yet behold two. Whilst I feel myself in sympathy with nature, & rejoice with divine greatly beating heart in the course of Justice & Benevolence overpowering me, I yet find little access to this Me of Me. (5:p. 337)

We might understand the "Me of Me" as temperament. According to "Experience," one has no command over one's temperament: it "enters fully into the system of illusions and shuts us in a prison of glass which we cannot see" (p. 53). The problem that persists is the lack of access to the divine choreographer. Within this scheme, the unity of the subject is clearly false.

How is this loss of integrity resolved? Emerson's solution is studied self-trust, informed consent to uphold the illusion of being that is ultimately constituted by the other. He wrote in the next lines of the journal entry:

> I behold; I bask in Beauty; I await; I wonder; Where is my Godhead now? This is the Male & Female principle in nature. One Man male & female created he him. Hard as it is to describe God it is harder to describe the Individual (p. 337).

The performance of subjectivity acts from the duality, the double-gendered entity of the "Godhead". Engendering the combination is not performed by the will to power as such, nor by the assumption of authority, but by willingness to be one with the other. The passage continues:

> A certain wandering light comes to me which I perceive to be the Cause of Causes. It transcends all proving. It is itself the ground of being, and I see that it is not one & I another (but) but this is the life of my life. That is one fact then that in certain moments I have known I existed directly from God, and am, as it were his organ. And in my ultimate consciousness Am he. Then, secondly, the contradictory fact is familiar, that I am a surprised spectator and learner all of my life. This is the habitual posture of the mind—, beholding. But whenever the day dawns, the great day of truth on the soul, it comes with

an awful invitation to me to accept it, to blend with its aurora (p. 337).

The "wandering light" is "the ground of being" that Emerson cannot prove, but apprehends as the part of him that precisely cedes his "I" in the phrase "Am he". He is not the subject, but a witness to his own becoming. The problem is that he must suffer experience not merely as a witness, but as one who relegates his imagined authority to the unknown, day after day. The individual is divided and conquered, yet she must trust herself to perform a kind of subjectivity that acts like a bluff. Emerson ends this remarkable passage with the troubled declaration "Can I not conceive of a universe without contradiction?" (p. 337) But it is precisely the duality of Janus-faced nature that permits a presumption of authority.

How does this work? If we take Alenka Zupančič's interpretation of Nietzsche's "Philosophy of The Two," understanding it as the elucidation of a creative potential within a temporal duality that is associated with language, we discern a multiplicity penetrable by pathos, which acts as a bridge, a transcending processual event. Figuratively, Zupančič's duality is the "edge"[91] between two planes in a multidimensional space, consisting of the difference composed of antithetical forces contained therein. In the dimensions of language, this axis acts like a copula—a term Emerson used to describe a sacred connection—that both links and distinguishes according to varying states of perception, performing a split between the individual and nature, abstracting a newly sensationalized "I". In other words, "the two" describes creative potential by framing pathos in the processual event, merging subject and object, authorizing the process of self-overcoming.

In Zupančič's frame, dynamic subjectivity occurs from beyond. Ariadne must become Dionysus through the medium of her affirmation. She must become other to herself in her assent to the "Thought" that is not her, that will become her. She becomes her own object. Thus Zupančič's formula, modeling Lacan's: Ariadne—Dionysus—Ariadne. She elaborates her theory by using the example of a declaration of love wherein language operates as the precipitating other.

---

91   Alenka Zupančič, The Shortest Shadow: Nietzsche's Philosophy of the Two (Boston: MIT Press, 2003): 12.

The event of love separates one with oneself through passion; one becomes outside of oneself. This break begets the amorous declaration in which language manifests as pathos. Its effect upon subjectivity is repercussive: a becoming oneself via the other, which first requires becoming other to oneself, is enacted. The split is a moment in which the "I" perishes—"I spoke my word, I break at my word, . . . as a proclaimer I perish"—and reforms.[92] Zupančič concludes that in this way "one became Two," or "'I' am two," and "'Nietzsche is two".[93] In the moment that the declaration occurs, there is a splintering from real to representational, wherein the representational becomes the medium of the real. The representation itself begets the real.

That Zupančič's declaration is "precipitated" associates it with Emersonian whim. As she explains, the declaration "involves a leap in causality not only in relation to the preexisting situation which it interrupts, but also in regard to its own begetting".[94] Like Emerson's saltatory thought, this leap of the mind in the universe occurs when language begets a reality of its own. This reasoning corroborates Emerson's theory of language in *Nature* and his conception of whim, whose derivation from "whimwham," or "fanciful object," identifies words as objects that are independent of the conscious mind. Whim is literally the ground-changing language of the event. According to Emerson's understanding of poiesis described in "Spiritual Laws," words must be affirmed, or manifested, in order to form the event. Ariadne's reception to the "clever word" bridges the split between her and Dionysus, actualizing pathos.

The Lover

In Nietzsche's writing, *amor fati* acts like Zupančič's declaration of love, merging the lover with the other by way of "a yea-saying to the point of justifying, to the point of redeeming even all that is past" (EH "Books" 8). The simple act of self-acceptance hinges on the apprehen-

---

92   Ibid., 12.

93   Ibid.,18.

94   Ibid.,12.

sion of one's innocence in the "terrible basic text homo natura" (BGE 230). Sarah Kofman understood this process as the affirmation of the "nakedness of Dionysus," conceptualized not as the figure stripped of its layers representing "Being in its truth," but as Nietzsche's self-over-coming.[95] Her reasoning involves Ariadne, who affirms the power of Dionysus by her wish to be loved by him. According to Kofman, Ariadne wanted to become "like the strong, handsome men" that Dionysus prefers.[96] But the notion that Ariadne wished to resemble a man would preclude her own self-overcoming. Derrida makes a similar error when he justified Nietzsche's disparagement of feminism.[97] The feminist does not wish to become like a man; rather, she seeks to obtain the same privileges. If we understand feminism as the organized effort to obtain political parity, we must acknowledge within feminism the simple claim to human rights, but Derrida dismisses this as mimicry. This kind of thinking denies woman as such, disdaining her claim to authenticity, thereby casting into doubt her ability to love.

In *The Epistles of Ovid*, Ariadne is a lover. The verse describes her longing for Theseus, who has abandoned her to serve the schemes of the gods. Dionysus pities her, marries her and makes her crown into the *Corona borealis*. "Ariadne's Lament" echoes the painful lamentation of Ovid's letter, but the aspect of the beloved is no longer Theseus, but he who regards her with "the spiteful lightning eyes of gods" (312). Rather than taking Ariadne as the lover of Theseus, Kofman understands her as Nietzsche's Ariadne, beloved of Dionysus, the god who imposes on her. The putative acquiescence of Nietzsche's Ariadne amounts to the acceptance of a fate that is not mediated by her own desires and indicates that her suffering, rather than her power, dignifies her.

We notice here that Nietzsche's valuation of suffering as the ultimate redemption is not inconsistent with Christian thought, but in his writing, it is the female that is sacrificed. Thus the style of *amor fati* bespeaks her agony: the "eternal feminine" comes across in the poem

---

95   Sarah Kofman, Nietzsche and Metaphor (Stanford, Stanford University Press, 1994): 97.

96   Ibid.

97   Derrida, Spurs, 43.

as the eternally-boring-in-Nietzsche, a return to his pedantic arrogance regarding women.

The image of the death-affirming female was familiar to Emerson: his eccentric aunt and mentor, Mary Moody Emerson, dressed daily in a shroud like the living symbol of *amor fati* (W 10:429). The difference between the two fatalistic female figures, apart from the fact that one was real and the other imagined, is that Mary Moody Emerson did not speak the recommended "Yes". She was an extraordinary nay-sayer, an imaginative and critical thinker who wrote volumes of letters to her nephew, excerpts of which appear in his essays attributed to the invented sage, Tunamarya, an acronym for Aunt Mary. Nietzsche's female, on the other hand, had neither the authority of language nor the dignity of self-possession.

Antinomian Women

Emerson envisioned the tragic heroine by the virtue of her antinomianism. Acknowledging the cultural context of Emersonian antinomianism as preceded by the Antinomian Controversy of the Massachusetts Bay Colony, described as the conflict between the biblical doctrines of grace and works, and considering the European history of the term that describes a dismantling of religious paradigms, we understand antinomianism as dramatic dissent that empowers justification over sanctification, or in Nietzsche's terms, willingness over will to power. What does antinomianism have to do with *amor fati*? By his declaration, Nietzsche affirmed love over legalism and spirit over language.

The antinomian females in Emerson's "Heroism" are Ariadne, Dorigen and his not-yet-tragic "fair girl". He offers another in his essay, "The Transcendentalist," in which Desdemona and Cato the Younger appear together as examples of the antinomian (p. 337). In Emerson's reasoning, Cato's suicide affirmed his honor, while Desdemona's honorable concealment of the identity of her murderer protected his. In other words, Cato sacrificed himself to guard his reputation but Desdemona was sacrificed in order to guard Othello's reputation. The comparison is outrageously misaligned. It expresses Emerson's patriarchal view of women, but also indirectly endorses violence against women, ratifying the claim Nietzsche made in *Beyond Good and Evil*, "*buona femmina e mala femmina vuol bastone* [the good and the bad woman wants a stick] Sacchetti, Nov. 86" (147). Emerson distanced himself from this interpretation by citing Jacobi, but he seems to have embraced the sense of it in "Heroism": the loyal woman who would die for love substantiates being. Clearly Emerson's affirmation of the female also required her suffering, though he imagined one whose sacrifice was not required.

Emerson did not endorse concrete female power in his works, but "Heroism" made the attempt to envision her potential, and in doing so, he conflated the female with both love and war, recommending a force that was antinomian in its essence, and potent in its process. Considering the struggles of the era during which Emerson wrote the essay—the abolitionist and suffragist movements—we understand the necessity of suffering as a condition for justice. The reference that he makes to the sacrifice of abolitionists in "Self Reliance," i.e., his naming of Lovejoy (202), points to the struggle at hand against slavery. Generally, his strongest language was reserved for this particular injustice. "The doctrine of hatred must be preached as the counteraction of the doctrine of love when that pules and whines" and "Thy love afar is spite at home" are uncharacteristically harsh judgements (51). Emerson's point was that self-proclaimed philanthropists who engaged against the economics of slavery abroad should instead attend to the evils of the "dismal science"[98] at home. The bloated sympathy that passes as love must be pricked by the sword of honest contempt to counter the complacency of the privileged. Emerson recommended at least the threat of war when conditions were intolerable.

Emerson's anti-pacifism in "Heroism" did not indicate a pro-war stance in general. West's sketch of him as hawk may have corrected the genteel interpretation, but it did not accurately describe the dynamics of his thought. In his description of Emerson, West cites Lopez, who miscites Emerson: "For Emerson, war was 'the Father of all things.'" Emerson actually wrote, "The old Greek Heraclitus

---

98   Thomas Carlyle, "Occasional Discourse on the Negro Question", Fraser's Magazine for Town and Country, Vol. XL., (1849): 670-679.

said, 'War is the Father of all things',"[99] in a speech on July 21, 1865, qualifying the citation: "He said it, no doubt, as science, but we of this day can repeat it as political and social truth" (343). The speech was addressed to a group of young veterans, for whom the legacy of war was self-evident. Lopez's assessment of Emersonian thought as "antagonizing"[100] ignores the moral force of this particular judgement: Emerson glorified the American Civil War not for its antagonism but because it "gave back integrity to this erring and immoral nation" (343). His celebration of the Civil War was extraordinary; not all wars can claim a similar justification.

Emerson's radical dualism was also not, as Paul Grimstad has argued, a form of compatibilism, which implies that there is no friction between the objects in a contradiction.[101] Fate and freewill do not merge or melt; their separate identities are crucial to their function. That there is an opposition between them is the defining structure for each. The "chiasmic unity" of fate and freewill expresses the nature of the Sphinx, in which struggle and suffering are necessary. Compatibilism attempts to eradicate the tragic world view, and in doing so, to sterilize the conception of the new.

Cavell understood Emersonian dualism as a kind of aversion that begets conversion. The aversion/conversion contradiction underwrites a persistent emotional value, offering a method for the philosopher, a "leaping free of enforced speech"[102] by way of imaginative interpretation that brings a writer closer to life. If philosophy asks how to live, Cavell suggests that Emerson's answer is seeking and finding and losing what is always already never actually had.

Desdemona, Dorigen and Ariadne operate in collusion with "the fair girl"—not to be confused with a *white* girl—as the affirmation of the tragic dimension of life. Their power is free of the intoxications of suffering because they are not actual women. Though Em-

---

99   As cited in West, American Evasion, 19.

100   Michael Lopez, "Emerson's Rhetoric of War." Prospects 12 (1987): 293–320.

101   Paul Grimstad, Experience and Experimental Writing: Literary Pragmatism from Emerson to the Jameses (Oxford: Oxford University Press, 2013).

102   Cavell "Founding as Finding," 140.

erson denounced the "interest" (2:480) of actual women in an early journal, perhaps referring to his avid friend Margaret Fuller, he publicly advocated for their political parity. His "fair girl" functioned as an ideal whose power was incipient. While Emerson's female had the possibility for autonomy, Nietzsche's ideal woman was meant to conform entirely to the other, acting as a love-slave.

Gay Sphinx

The "manliness" that Stack identified as a controlling passion for both Emerson and Nietzsche was code for "greatness".[103]   The quality did not exclude women on principle for Nietzsche, who wrote, in *The Gay Science*, "Great man - From the fact that someone is a 'great man' one cannot infer that he is a man; he may be just a boy, or a chameleon of all stages of life, or a bewitched little woman" (208). The "bewitched little woman" seems to be of the same species as the magical women who appear earlier in the book, but she comes across as more human, or at least more male. But the privileging of maleness is also understood as an illusion, wrought by a master-slave morality: "The 'great men,' as they are reverenced, are poor little fictions composed afterwards" (BGE 269). In this section of *Beyond Good and Evil*, great women are also targets of Nietzsche's ire: the "eternal feminine" becomes "the eternally-boring-in-woman" (323). "Feminine scientificality" (323) saps the life of his romantic female figure.

Dismantle the eternal feminine and one finds Nietzsche's "twin soul," who can be heard from behind the stage curtains in *The Gay Science* as the "alto voice" that speaks of "Women who master their masters": "with lofty, heroic, royal souls, capable of and ready for grandiose retorts, resolutions, and sacrifices, capable of and ready for mastery over men, because in them the best of man aside from his sex has become an incarnate ideal" (70). This seems to be another reference to Emerson's "fair girl". Again, Nietzsche rejects these characters as implausible: when they perform, their voices retain "motherly and housewifely coloring" (70). Like the "unsuccessful ones" in a subsequent aphorism, their voices fail to seduce. The winning charm of Ni-

---

103   Stack, *Emerson & Nietzsche*, 311.

etzsche's "bewitched little woman" might be her "clairvoyance in the world of suffering" (BGE 208). She is passionate, and if she passes as "great," it's probably because she seems cheerful. For both Nietzsche and Emerson, a woman's happiness was her redemption: she was less pitiable for it.

A century before Nietzsche wrote the first edition of *The Gay Science*, Germaine de Staël published a treatise on the science of happiness, entitled *The Influence of The Passions on Individuals and Nations*, in which she classified the impassioned as doomed, arguing that happiness can only be arrived at through a sort of refined nonchalance, exactly like the cabbage-brained moderns that Nietzsche deplored. In her reasoning, women—whom she claimed are by nature more excitable and impulsive than men—seem to suffer excessively from their devotion. Their happiness is not easily attained owing to their romantic tendencies. Passionate happiness, de Staël wrote, is impossible to sustain. She recommended impassivity, presuming that love is sacrifice of self.[104] Nietzsche disagreed: his love, like Emerson's, implicated the self rather than sacrificing it. For both writers, the passionate character who eschewed self-pity and pity itself was the true lover. Compassion was taken as a given.

Everlasting Transformation

Nietzsche's ideal feminine constitutes an eternal return to Ariadne. His major female characters, not counting "woman as such," and in order of their appearance, are the "silent, magical creatures" (60) and "bewitched little woman" (70) of *The Gay Science*; the Sphinx of *Beyond Good and Evil*; Baubo of the second edition of *The Gay Science*; and both Ariadne's, the first of the "Dionysian Dithyrambs," and the second of *Ecce Homo* 4. In this sequence, the charmers yield to the monster who is disarmed by the comic who defers to the divine. Del Caro points to Cosima Wagner, wife of Richard Wagner and

---

104   Madame de Staël (Anne-Louise-Germaine), *A Treatise on the Influence of the Passions Upon the Happiness of Individuals and Nations: Illustrated by Striking References to the French Revolution* (G. Cawthorn, British Library, 1798).

mother of his children, as the actual identity of Ariadne.[105] Perhaps
the long-suffering Cosima, whom Nietzsche addressed as Ariadne in
a letter written to her late in his life, and with whom he had long con-
versations in the afternoons of his Wagner admiration, was the living
symbol of Ariadne. But Nietzsche's symbolic female figures, with the
exception of Baubo—who seems to be Nietzsche in disguise—can all
be traced to Emerson.

Cavell's intuition of a likeness between Emerson and Nietzsche
came about by the "Emersonian master tones"[106] that he heard in Nietzsche's writing. A deeper connection revolves around a poetics of allusion. Del Caro directs us to Nietzsche's use of allusion as a universal
principle in *Human All Too Human*:

> No new substances and characters, but the old, long-familiar
> in everlasting new order and transformation: that is the art, as
> Goethe later did, as the Greeks, and indeed the French, prac-
> ticed it (221).

But Nietzsche actually does introduce a new character, The Overman,
with his central message of eternal recurrence. Like the "genius of
the heart," the Overman is nameless. If Emerson was the model for
the Overman, which Nietzsche read in "Power" as the "Uberschuss-
mensch" (Fabricus' translation of the "plus man"), then the Overman
is not new but novelistic, akin to his great men who are fictions composed afterwards.

Del Caro's assessment that "very little is to be gained from try-
ing to guess just who Nietzsche had in mind each time he wrote something"[107] ignores the interpretive possibilities conjured by Nietzsche's
reading of Emerson. Examination of their shared allusions illuminates Nietzsche's considerations as he resisted and took in Emerson's
ideas, reflecting back on the original. Context always qualifies. One
may want one's Nietzsche in the clouds as a "pathos of distance" (GM

---

105   Del Caro, "Symbolizing Philosophy: Ariadne and The Labyrinth," Nietzsche Studien 17 no. 1 (1988): 149.

106   Cavell, "Old and New in Emerson and Nietzsche," 225.

107   Del Caro,"Symbolizing Philosophy," 149.

I:2) but situating his work within a frame of reference can make sense of his egregious claims about the female gender. Whether the text can perform in dimensions that hold it true to itself is the rather important question for the female reader of Nietzsche, whose self-identification as the hated object turns her against herself on one of these dimensions.

It seems that in the end, Nietzsche's inclination was to educate. He would first teach men to instruct women to be "willful," (GS 68) then teach woman "to learn to hate herself so she can love herself,"(48) in order to increase her courage, like the gods in Plato's *Laws* who trained their warriors by administering a poison that causes fear so that they could learn to overcome its effects. While his stance towards women was not as plainly encouraging as Emerson's, his writing corroborates a metalanguage that dignifies his female reader, demanding from her a kind of confidence.

Part IV.

CIRCLES

A(morality)

Emerson and Nietzsche teach critical thinking and self-trust, mediated by an energy that exceeds itself, expressed in the spirit of play. Emerson's harmonizing instinct, the moral sentiment, was problematic for Nietzsche, but can be clarified by the meaning of *amor fati*. Yes-saying to the burgeoning self as it corresponds to the multiplicity involves the repudiation of shame, the affirmation of grace, and an Aristotelian conflation of the good with the beautiful. This kind of morality is only possible with a belief in morality, an acceptance of the possibility of benevolence.

Morality for Nietzsche was implausible, his natural aversion notwithstanding. It is not accurate to say that he was a nihilist. Anarchy for anarchy's sake was not the freedom he sought, and he made this clear in *The Gay Science* with the proposition of a better, more humorous humanity negotiated through honest reckoning. His chief immoralist, introduced at the end of the book, is described in *Ecce Homo* as a stylized version of the historical *Zarathustra*, the prophet who redeemed "truthfulness":

> *Zarathustra* created this most calamitous error, morality; consequently, he must also be the first to recognize it. [...] His doctrine, and his alone, posits truthfulness as the highest virtue; this means the opposite of the cowardice of the "idealist" who flees from reality [...]—Am I understood?— The self-overcoming of morality, out of truthfulness; the self-overcoming of the moralist, into his opposite—into me—that is what the name of *Zarathustra* means in my mouth ("Why I Am a Destiny", 3).

As the missionary for immoralism, Nietzsche's fictional *Zarathustra* seeks to redeem morality by invigorating its honesty. By examining and accepting ourselves as we are—not held against ideals of virtue— we may begin to see where our justification lies: in the love that elevates a humble life. Over and over again, *Zarathustra* preaches love: "I love him for he seeks to create beyond himself" (16:4). A scrupulous evaluation of human motivation that is not beholden to the religious imperative to sanctify human worth conducts a transcendence of morality that reinvigorates the real.

Friend of Noon

Nietzsche understood his work—the attempt to redress the question of good and evil by exposing a morality whose roots had become effectively detached from their origins by its proclamation alone— as a development of the historical *Zarathustra*'s work. He imagined that the spirit of the ancient Persian prophet overtook him on a mountain path, and spoke through him as if to true "the essential wheel in the workings of things"[108] in the struggle between good and evil. The bulk of the writing of *Thus Spake Zarathustra* was completed in ten days; he was clearly inspired.

The inspiration for *Zarathustra* came to Nietzsche on the peak of a mountain at midday, an event that he describes in the poem "From High Mountains," published as the Aftersong to *Beyond Good and Evil*. What happened during this wandering moment of self-overcoming? The last stanza of the poem announces the arrival of *Zarathustra*, but the penultimate stanza refers to a mysterious character who was responsible for the death of Nietzsche's misery:

> This song is over—the sweet cry of longing
> > Died in my mouth—
> A sorcerer did it, the friend at the right time,
> The friend of noon—no! do not ask who he is—
> At noon was the time one became two ..
>
> Now we celebrate together, certain of victory,
> > The feast of feasts:
> Friend *Zarathustra* has come, the guest of guests!
> Now the world laughs, the dread curtain is rent,
> The wedding has come for light and darkness .....

---

108   Nietzsche, as cited by Elizabeth Forster-Nietzsche in her Introduction to *Thus Spake Zarathustra*, xxii.

The one that was Nietzsche becomes the two of Nietzsche-Zarathus-tra, the celebrants of the last stanza. Zarathustra is clearly identified as "the guest of guests," but Nietzsche's reference to the mysterious "friend at the right time'" begs the question: who brought Zarathustra to Nietzsche's feast? The metaphors that he used immediately suggest that it was Emerson. The brief opening paragraph of Emerson's essay "Circles," which Nietzsche read closely, ends dramatically with the line "there is always another dawn risen on mid-noon and under every deep a lower deep opens," (302) the first clause of which Emerson cribbed from John Milton's "Paradise Lost". In the fourth paragraph of the essay, Emerson describes a "wheel without wheel" that is moved by "the force of truth of the individual soul," (305) a metaphor that resembles "the essential wheel in the working of things" that Nietzsche associated with Zarathustra. Was Nietzsche's Sphinx-brother, his "twin-soul," his "genius of the heart," his dancing god, also his "friend of noon"?

At the same time that he was working on *Zarathustra* and preparing *Beyond Good and Evil*, according to Walter Kaufmann in the preface to his translation of *The Gay Science*, Nietzsche came across a reference to "a certain poet," whom Kaufmann suspected might have been "the Magian," or Zoroaster.[109] Emerson referred to Zarathustra by his Greek name throughout his works. The lines that Kaufmann cites—"'Man is a dwarf of himself'" and "'A man is a god in ruins'"— sound like Nietzsche, he wrote, but were attributed to Emerson's "Orphic Poet". "Was this perhaps the seed of *Thus Spoke Zarathustra?*" Kaufmann asks. But, according to the "Pan. Divine Seed" heading of Emerson's 1836 Journal, the lines attributed to "a certain poet" were recollected fragments of his conversation with Bronson Alcott (4:78). The "Orphic Poet" was not Zoroaster, but Emerson's boisterous and silly neighbor, a man who couldn't remember much of what anyone said, but rejoiced in speaking himself. Alcott's "Orphic Sayings" were gleefully mocked by his contemporaries; the New York Knickerbocker parodied them as "The Gastric Sayings".[110] Thomas Carlyle called

---

109   Kaufmann, Nietzsche, 263.

110   As cited in Packer, Barbara (2007). The Transcendentalists. Athens, Georgia: The University of Georgia Press. And: Knickerbocker (12)volume 16 issue 5 (November 1840) 452.

him "a kind of Venerable Don Quixote, whom nobody can laugh at without loving".[111]

Nietzsche certainly came across several references to Zoroaster in his reading of the *Versuche*, but whether or not Zarathustra entered Nietzsche's mindscape via Emerson would be difficult to prove, considering that translations of the Gathas were available in German at the time. Emerson may or may not have been "the friend of noon," though it seems that he was. What is clear is that his emphasis on honesty offered Nietzsche a remedy to the wobbling course of Christian morality.

Destiny of the Oversoul

Nietzsche's new morality was grounded in a tentative benevolence in nature whose code was antinomian. This morality as anti-morality esteemed the body and its instincts. Its earth-bound ethos echoed the commandments of the Crows, the Lakotas and other Native American Tribes. The character of the new morality was the Overman, introduced in the last lines in the addended Book V of *The Gay Science*:

> Another ideal runs ahead of us... the ideal of a human, superhuman well-being and benevolence that will often appear inhuman-for example, when it confronts all earthly seriousness so far, all solemnity in gesture, word, tone, eye, morality, and task so far, as if it were their most incarnate and involuntary parody-and in spite of all of this, it is perhaps only with him that great seriousness really begins, that the real question mark is posed for the first time, that the destiny of the soul changes, the hand moves forward, the tragedy begins (382).

These lines are taken to be an introduction to the novel in which the Overman is prophesied as a human ideal.

---

111   As cited in Whipple, "Emerson and Carlyle." North American 439. The North American Review , May, 1883, Vol. 136, No. 318 (May, 1883),431- 445.

The theory of the Overman was diagrammed in the *Nachlass* as a consolation for the misery of eternal recurrence provoked by the death of God: the "sacred murder" (10:4:132) unleashes the possibility of self-determination by way of acquiescence to fate. In his outline, Nietzsche described hermits who imagined the "smile of the dying" (10:4:132) on the beatific front of a suffering Zarathustra who has lost all severity, evoking the enigma of the beyond-man: "(As God lives) God is dead, and it is time for the overman to live" (10:4:132). If, like Schrödinger's cat, God is both alive and dead, the proclamation of *amor fati* as it relates to eternal recurrence invites mortals to create their own destiny, even as their tragedy—the loss of their immortality—is inevitable.

The question that has to be confronted, given the argument that Nietzsche's revaluations were rooted in his reading of the *Versuche*, is whether "The Oversoul" was the source of Nietzsche's Overman. It is not a stretch to associate the Overman with the Oversoul, considering that Emerson's essay was closely read by Nietzsche, who left excited marks, notes and underlining in lead and red pencil alongside the text. In "The Oversoul," Emerson did not commit "the sacred murder" directly, but he recommended a break-up.†5   It was clear to him that the second coming had not occurred and in the meantime, the promise of the first had flickered out. Heraclitan fire ignited scriptural mysteries: the absolute authority of Christianity was replaced by the animation of nature.

"The Oversoul" describes a world that has been spiritualized by the cultivation of human nature through love. The divinity at hand is not the God of Abraham, Mohammed nor Jesus, nor any other prophet but oneself, and we are drawn to others in whom we recognize the divine faculty. Emerson's statement, "I am certified of a common nature," (p. 277) affirms an aspiring, justice-seeking humanity composed of "separate selves" (p. 277). The union of these selves constructs a society that "arches over like a temple" with "higher self-possession" (p. 278). Wisdom is regard for what is true, and what is true reveals itself. The lauded scholar might not be privy to the winning insight of a simpleton; though he may pursue the truth with "the violence of direction," (279) his probing assails instinctual truth. Not thinking but

---

†5

intense feeling, felt in moments that redeem eons of meanness, opens the universal mind. In short, the "soul of the whole; the wise silence; the universal beauty," (p. 270) a phrase that Nietzsche underlined in his reading, are the powers that "fire the heart" (p. 293) of this revolutionary metaphysical imagination.

In an earlier essay, "The Method of Nature," Emerson associated the cultivation of a collaborative, visionary, and enlightened humanity with Zoroaster:

> It is remarkable that we have, out of the deeps of antiquity in the oracles ascribed to the half fabulous Zoroaster, a statement of this fact which every lover and seeker of truth will recognize. "It is not proper," said Zoroaster, "to understand the Intelligible with vehemence, but if you incline your mind, you will apprehend it: not too earnestly, but bringing a pure and inquiring eye. You will not understand it as when understanding some particular thing, but with the flower of the mind. Things divine are not attainable by mortals who understand sensual things, but only the light-armed arrive at the summit" (214-15).

The emphasis on a truth that is available to those who can see with "the flower of the mind" rather than with "vehemence" of determination is consistent with the aesthetical ethics of "The Oversoul," indicating that Emerson connected his Oversoul with the teachings of Zarathustra.

Budding Man

Nietzsche's marginalia in "The Oversoul" point to Emerson as the origin of the Overman. On the top of page 205 in his copy of the *Versuche*, he wrote this enigmatic note:

> The real man is far behind the embryonic, which emerges from him only in three generations.

Further on this page, Emerson describes the ubiquity of the Oversoul: "As it is present in all persons, so it is in every period of life. It is adult already in the infant man" (p. 280). Nietzsche read "Schön im angehenden Menschen ist es ausgebildet," with Fabricus' translation of "infant" as "angehenden," i.e. budding.[113]   We can interpret the budding man as Nietzsche's "embryonic" man from which the "real man" emerged in three generations, directly connecting Nietzsche's Overman with Emerson's Oversoul.

One might imagine the Overman as the manifestation of the Oversoul, suitably proposed as a fiction. But such a fiction contorts the meaning of the Oversoul, which is never just one. The Oversoul cannot be reduced to an individual: it is always a multiplicity. If the multiplicity is understood as the one, or in the one, as in Nietzsche's pluralized subjectivity, then the Overman can be understood as a manifestation of the Oversoul. But in *Zarathustra*, this is unclear: his proclamations emphasize a singularity.

The singularity of the Overman, that is, the character of the Overman, was plausibly inspired by the character of Emerson. The aloof but silly genius that Nietzsche encountered in his *Versuche* is easily a model for the figure who teaches love, honesty and contempt. If the Overman is the dancing god, the philosophical ideal that Nietzsche described at the end of *The Gay Science*, then the Overman as "the ideal of a human, superhuman well-being and benevolence" (382) clearly came from Emerson. What is at the heart of this philosophical enterprise is an education in a more daring morality: "One must learn to love" (334).

Learning to Love

Love for Nietzsche is a charged polarity that includes hate; it is always a part of nature and is entangled in the concept of woman who is wound in life, truth and wisdom. Love is not an object, but the

---

113   Digitale Sammlungen der Herzogen Anna Amalia Bibliothek gallery of Nietzsche's copy of Emerson's Versuche, Aus dem Englisch von G. Fabricus: https://haab-digital.klassik-stiftung.de/viewer/image/118058662X/8/LOG_0002/
Or: https://global.oup.com/us/companion.websites/9780190929213/ap/

medium of the world. There is no equality in love. Nietzsche indicates that though love and morality are incompatible, the love that grounds Dionysian pessimism is conscientious in that it does not seek revenge. Even as the conditions of love are contradictory and potentially destructive, an effort to engage is worth its pains:

> In the end we are always rewarded for our good will, our patience, fairmindedness, and gentleness with what is strange; gradually, it sheds its veil and turns out to be a new and indescribable beauty. That is its thanks for our hospitality. Even those who love themselves will have learned it in this way; for there is no other way. Love. too, has to be learned (GS 334).

As a future orientation, this sort of conscience requires the acceptance of the possibility of benevolence as the truth itself.

Nietzsche entertains the idea of benevolence in *The Gay Science* with some trepidation, but in "Schopenhauer as Educator," a work in which Emerson is asserted tacitly as a moral example exceeding that of Schopenhauer, he sounds committed:

> It is love alone that can bestow on the soul, not only a clear, discriminating, self-contemptuous view of itself, but also a desire to look beyond itself, and to seek with all its might for a higher self as yet still concealed from it (6).

In the essay, Nietzsche explicitly criticizes Schopenhauer for his lack of love, †8 implying that he failed to instruct the good life. The desire to help mankind correct errors was written in Schopenhauer, Nietzsche observed, but his ethic was as unpromising as the Stoic sensibility: it made of man a statue. Provocation is the best teacher, as Emerson wrote, and though Schopenhauer may have been his educator, Emerson provoked him with infernal optimism. Nietzsche rejected Emersonian optimism—perhaps substituting optimism with the more temperamental cheerfulness—but not his valuation of love.

It seems that for Nietzsche learning to love involved learning to see, but "it is impossible to teach love" (6). The love that cannot be taught but has to be learned makes life worth living only through the grace of "our hospitality" towards our inevitable selves as well as those for whom we feel contempt. In *Ecce Homo* Nietzsche offers an explicit definition of love as it relates to woman:

> Have people had ears to hear my definition of love? It is the only definition worthy of a philosopher. Love, in its means, is war; in its foundation, it is the mortal hatred of the sexes (5).

If the proclamation of a war between the sexes implies a sense of dispossession, and the accompanying desire to possess, war is a masculine affair. Nietzsche's feminine love, described in GS 363 as the desire to be possessed, affirms willingness, but his masculine love, as the desire to possess, describes the will to power, the desire to own one's fate, i.e., self-determination by way of struggle. In the political field, we understand the declaration of war as encompassing both masculine and feminine self-interests as a mode of reclaiming possession of what has been transgressed upon. The female desire to claim power in the political field indicates that her interests are like his: she also desires to possess. In other words, female will to power is also a manner of self-determination.

What stands out here is love as a process. One cannot simply eradicate the problem of love—the greedy desire to possess—but one can attempt to overcome it. The sublimation of desire and its chaos of instincts serve the propensity for critical thinking. In *Twilight*, Nietzsche provides another definition of love that introduces it as an intellectual ideal that emerges from the body: "the spiritualization of sensuality is love" ("Morality as Anti-nature" 4). This love presents as educated Eros, an abstract affection that instructs the Dionysian instinct.

To appreciate the redemption of the body by both Nietzsche and Emerson, one must understand the destructive force of bad conscience. According to Kaufmann's reading of Nietzsche, man "must first develop the feeling that his impulses are evil;" he must "burn a No into his own soul".[115] To redeem the body, a person must validate it, in effect searing a Yes in place of the branded No. This rehabilitation of impulses attempts to redress learned actions

---

115   Kaufmann, *Nietzsche*, 263.

that have become involuntary through repetition, a kind of training that effectively cultivates conscience.

Moral Sentiment

Emerson's "moral sentiment" is synonymous with the kind of conscience that demands action. His idea was informed by David Hartley's early attempt at formulating neurological origins of moral psychology.[116] Hartley's process described a unity between the "infinitesimal parts"[117] of things that interact with the mind to form ideas in a neurobiology of nature. This cogency is the physiological mechanism of the moral sentiment, which involves "diachronic improvisation," a function of "decomplex"[118] actions that are in fact extremely complex. A "diachronic improvisation" is a voluntary action that is performed automatically. When involuntary knowledge has been internalized through repetition or training, as in a music recital, memory is no longer called upon consciously; intermediaries like the notes of music are unnecessary for performance. Learned actions become diachronic by the transference of voluntary knowledge to involuntary knowledge, as in the defensive gesture of one accustomed to being struck.

Hartley's unification of consciousness conceptualized "decomplex" actions in the physiology of animals, not limiting it to humans. The concept was extended to all organic substances by way of Hartley's collaborator, Steven Hales, who theorized that nature is composed of forces of attraction and repulsion that seek

---

116   David Hartley, Observations on Man, His Frame, His Duty, and His Expectations, (OM) (Cambridge: Cambridge University Press), 46.

117   Hartley called this "joint impression," which effects "association:" "Since therefore sensations are conveyed to the mind, by the efficiency of corporeal causes … it seems to me, that the powers of generating ideas, and raising them by association, must also arise from corporeal causes, and consequently admit of an explication from the subtle influences of the small parts of matter on each other, as soon as these are sufficiently understood." Hartley (OM 1, prop 11).

118   Hartley, OM 1, prop 12.

balance.[119]   Hartley applied this concept to moral psychology by way of "associations" and "counter associations".[120]   The disjunction in forgetting, detachment or loss of consciousness (like sleep) breaks the continuity of association to balance the mind, so that it is "maintained in a continual round of the production and dissolution".[121]   Without the dissolution, there would be no learning, as associations would be continuously generated, undiscerned and indiscernible. In this sense, Hartley's nature is pure discernment, embodied as conscience, which acts like the moral sentiment as "a rapid intrinsic energy" that "worketh everywhere, righting wrongs, correcting appearances, and bringing up facts to a harmony with thoughts" (W 1:127).

In his journal, Emerson praised Sir James Macintosh's exposition of Hartley's work for having provided a novel definition of conscience, but he rejected Macintosh's own *Ethics* for its classification of conscience as a secondary formation (2:470). Emerson understood the moral impulse as primary formation, and preferred the hospitable ambiguity of the term "moral sentiment" to Macintosh's conscience, which perhaps had been ruined for him in Hamlet. By paralyzing action, Macintosh's legalistic conscience and Hamlet's agonizing conscience exude all the strength of a mallet and none of the force of nature that Emerson's term proposes. Likewise, Emerson's moral sentiment was dissimilar to Adam Smith's, with which he was familiar (W 10:421). Though both affirmed the authority of common sense, Smith's estimation of love—he called it "ridiculous"[122] —did not accord with Emerson's.

Joseph Urbas contends that the moral sentiment was grounded in metaphysics and as such is dissimilar to the "moral perfectionism" to which Cavell likens it.[123]   Urbas is right to stress a metaphysical aspect.

---

119   Stephen Hales, Statical Essays: containing Haemastatics; Or, An Account of some Hydraulic and Hydrostatical Experiments made on the Blood and Blood-Vessels of Animals (London: Wilson and Nichol, Keith, Robinson and Roberts, 1769).

120   Hartley, OM 1, prop. 91.

121   Ibid.

122   Adam Smith, The Theory of Moral Sentiments, III ii, 2.

123   Joseph Urbas, "Cavell 'Moral Perfectionism' or Emerson's 'Moral Senti-

Emerson also called the moral sentiment the "religious sentiment," (W 1:125) tracing it to the East:

> The moral sentiment...dwelled always deepest in the minds of men in the devout and contemplative East; not alone in Palestine, where it reached its purest expression, but in Egypt, in Persia, in India, in China. Europe has always owed to oriental genius its divine impulses. What these holy bards said, all sane men found agreeable and true (127).

Emerson synthesized the values he encountered in his studies of various religions, and summarized them by using the term. But the term is more physical than metaphysical. The moral sentiment as the designation of right action is immediate. It does not concern an afterlife, a concept that has no play with Emerson.

In his "Ethnical Scriptures" column in *The Dial*, Emerson translated religious texts from mostly Asian sources—Islam, Hinduism, Sikhism, Zoroastrianism—featuring values that resonated with the American Transcendentalists, who were profoundly influenced by the Quakers.[124] In a journal entry from May 7, 1832, he wrote "in the language of William Penn, moral sentiment is called Christ" (4:14). The context of the entry, headed by the phrase "*Mutato nomine de te fabula narratur*," reveals the service of the term: Change the name and the tale is told of you. Principles present in a variety of religious narratives were affirmed by the moral sentiment, which always provides the answer to the question "What is the right thing to do"? The response to the question finds itself as active or passive.

We have acknowledged that Emerson is filled with many gods, while paying tribute to the authoritative deity in New England at the time. Calvin's God, ignited by the inner spirits of the Quaker divinity, infused conscience with the moral sentiment. Enthusiasm, divine presence, or love as the cause of revelation in a body could enact an increase in awareness whose positive charge produced an universal orientation, unlike the God of Abraham. The question of whether

---

ment'," in European Journal of Pragmatism and American Philosophy, II 2, 2010.

124   Sarina Isenberg, "Translating World Religions, Ralph Waldo Emerson and Henry David Thoreau's 'Ethnical Scriptures' column in The Dial," in Comparative American Studies: An International Journal (Volume 11: I, 2013), 18-36.

Emerson meant to diminish the significance of traditional Christian worship in his environs to cede way for a physical apprehension of the divine by preaching allegiance to a metaphysical interaction between nature and the Individual is answered in Emerson's verse, indeed, in his entire works. The epigraphical poem to "History" shows us that Emerson would combine and prescribe divine elements, even those less than divine like Shakespeare and Caesar, and abolish nothing (2). Emerson did not remove idols from their pedestals, but crowded them there with other idols. There was no ultimate ideal but the value of human participation in nature as a way of becoming true in a cosmos that is infiltrated with personality: gods with style, gods with hammers, gods with three faces, female gods with excellence, knowledge and scrupulousness.

The Nameless

What cohered with Emerson is what was affirmed; for this reason, he took pains to affirm the negation. In "Experience" more than any other essay, Emerson seems to have "drunk and seen the spider" as Leontes does in *A Winter's Tale*. His knowledge of the world had been infected, perhaps by his own perception. In this way, the authority in "Experience" is self-directed and self-blaming. Responsibility for his claims in *Nature* are taken personally, and in the essay, we hear the ruminations of conscience.

Cavell makes the comparison between Emerson's "Experience" and *A Winter's Tale* on the basis of the death of a son, and the father's sense of complicity in his son's death.[125] As Cavell focuses on the "buried" Waldo at the core of "Experience," he cites Emerson: "For contact with reality, we would even pay the costly price of sons and lovers," (W 3:48) and then draws the comparison to Shakespeare's play "in which the death of a son and a loving wife are the cost for the refusal to recognize contact with the reality of a birth".[126] This contact would be with the "nameless," or what Emerson later calls "Be-

---

125   Stanley Cavell, "Finding as Founding," 119.

126   Ibid., 126.

ing". Cavell asks "Is the genius-essayist of 'Experience' representing the cause that refuses to be named, by the emphatic representation of a dead son whose passing he cannot get nearer to him?"[127]   He does not immediately grapple with the question, rather he refocuses on Emersonian "generalization," which he defines as propagation by likening the term to "genesis" in the Emersonian paradigm of begetting new circles. But he asks again a few lines later, "Is the correct identification of Waldo the emphatic symbol of being?"[128] In other words, is the lost child one of Emerson's "Lords of succession," connected with his relegation of divine "reality"? Cavell here either associates the nameless cause with the love of a father for his son, or with the identity of father with son. Are the father and the son the same Waldo? Is Cavell reading a Kantian succession? Because of the emphasis on sentiment, it seems more likely that Waldo, the nameless and unchanging cause in Cavell's construction, signals generalized love, Waldo buried in the writing as genesis.

One question to ask would be: where is the becoming in this view, when the subject is no longer obvious? An answer might be found in Nietzsche's writing from the *Nachlass* that refers to problems with the illusory nature of perception as it relates to knowledge, which describes "a world of becoming" that "could not, in a strict sense, be 'grasped'". Our knowledge is "an illusion" of "preserved life," much like the surprising appearance of Hermione at the end of *A Winter's Tale* as a statue brought back to life in a gesture of magical realism (36[26]). How this works for Nietzsche is expressed in the next entry of his notebook:

> Philosophy in the only way I still allow it to stand, as the most general form of history, as an attempt somehow to describe Heraclitean becoming and to abbreviate it into signs (so to speak, to translate and mummify it into a kind of illusory being) (36[27]).

---

127   Ibid.

128   Ibid.

Becoming becomes encrypted in the language of philosophy. Why not the language of poetry? For Nietzsche, poetry has been infected by women: the greatest poets are "men of the moment, sensual, absurd, fivefold, irresponsible, and sudden in mistrust and trust" (UM "Wagner" 2). For Emerson, poetry is a designation of "occult symmetries," while philosophy is Heraclitan "dry light" that casts outward. Philosophy seeks to help others by structuring sentiment through the mechanism of critical thinking, as Emerson explains in "Experience". His revision in "The Scholar" of the precise nature of the "Joyous Science" from its original designation as poetry to its secondary designation as scholarship occurred after the death of his son, indicating that his experience taught him to appreciate "Being" as the strife involved in learning rather than the rapture of discovery.

Honey Sacrifice

The formation of a new philosophy is the question that Nietzsche considers in "Schopenhauer as Educator," wherein he presents an aesthetic justification of being and rejection of becoming. The question of what one is can only be answered by "being in the imperishable" (4) as pathos. His later works confirm that mere contentment was not his end: Zarathustra's advice, "Become what you are," disdains happiness in favor of the strife involved with upholding "Being" as a real. Zarathustra's "Honey Sacrifice" is not actually a sacrifice but a ruse: his cheerfulness transforms into a lure meant to attract "the finest human fish," (IV 61) who can experience joy beyond contentment. Nietzsche explicitly rejects the ascetic ideal in *The Genealogy of Morals*, where the ascetic is presented as a spiritualized dogmatist whose proposition of nothingness is as senseless as the Christian's faith in God. Nietzsche calls this position "dignified philosophic abstinence" (24). This "wish for standing still in front of the actual" (24) describes a stoic orientation that is declined in the statement of *amor fati* as suffering for the other. Passion is the axis of *amor fati*, and Nietzsche generally dismissed Stoicism for its lack of passion, (BGE 9) though the stoic art of suffering—along with "Russian fatalism" (EH "Wise" 6) and Buddhism (AC 20)—are practices that Nietzsche defended as therapeutic.

For Nietzsche, the death of God meant freedom from the immorality seeded in traditional metaphysics, and freedom for the possibilities of honest self-determination, the real morality. To affirm oneself honestly means to play with the possibilities of the present. In this sense, *amor fati* is understood as the mitigation of "Being" expressed ecstatically. Nietzsche describes the new philosopher as a levitating being for whom:

> the earth loses its gravity, the events and powers of the earth become dreamlike, transfiguration spreads itself about him as on summer evenings. To him who sees these things it is as though he were just beginning to awaken and what is playing about him is only the clouds of a vanishing dream (4).

The ecstatic moment validates the metaphysical sensibility, associated with the female in the "vita femina" (GS 339), who is elsewhere a symbol of deception. Despite Nietzsche's atheism, his "formula for greatness" (EH "Clever" 10) confirms a metaphysical orientation.

Likewise, despite his polemics against morality, Nietzsche affirmed virtue as a foundational power. He articulated this view in *Will to Power*:

> When morality—that is to say subtlety, caution, bravery, equity— has been as it were stored through the practice of a whole succession of generations, then the total force of this accumulation of virtue radiates even into that sphere where integrity is most seldom found, into the spiritual sphere (440).

In other words, if morality can be spiritualized through gradual transformation—if the scions of "subtlety, caution, bravery, equity" can be cultivated in a process that looks like karma and acts like the Oversoul—the spiritual estate of accumulated benevolence can be freed in the experiment of becoming, so that pathos effectively serves ethos. The passage continues:

> Genius resides in instinct; goodness likewise. One acts perfectly only when one acts instinctively. Even from the

viewpoint of morality, all conscious thinking is merely tentative, usually the reverse of morality (440).

Nietzsche's ideas were clearly influenced by Emerson. If both genius
and goodness are located in the body, its whims and instincts can be
understood as the agents of intelligence and morality. Intentionality, or
rather, the interference of conscious thought, might actually obstruct
ethical action. Nietzsche's affirmation of the moral sentiment emphasized the limitations of rationality in a trajectory that forges the future.

Greatest Theory in Use

Amor fati in an Emersonian sense involves heeding oneself in a
complex: the one is always part of the many. When a person's actions
and behavior accord with her character, she affirms the complexity of
the Oversoul. This process of trusting oneself encourages "a little
whim of will to be free/gallantly contending against the universe of
chemistry," (W 6:30) which permits conscience and circumstance to
coincide in the enactment of becoming. In other words, one is ethically self-determined in this process: a person can construct herself
within the confines inscribed in what Nietzsche calls fate and Emerson
terms the "Beautiful Necessity".

Emersonian fatalism commits to play, or experiment, rather
than to victory against the Fates. There is an emphasis on knowing
how to be a fatalist, learning how to cultivate whim, or to proceed with
a kind of impulse that is not murderous. He qualified the connection
between common fatalism and refined fatalism in his letter to Caroline
Sturgis, July 22, 1853:

> Fatalism, foolish & flippant, is as bad as unitarianism or Mor-
> monism. But fatalism held by an intelligent soul who knows
> how to humor & obey the infinitesimal pulses of spontaneity
> is by much the greatest theory in use. All the great would
> call their thought fatalism, or concede that ninety nine parts
> are nature, & one part power, though that hundredth is
> elastic, miraculous, and, whenever it is in energy, dissolving all
> the rest (L 4:3).

Whim, as obedience to "the infinitesimal pulses of spontaneity," is understood as an improvisation that requires a willingness to perform in a way that is not prescribed or intended, revoking the blind tyranny of will to power in favor of an allegiance to nature. Will is overcome by whim, the source of which is greater than the self, by which the self is possessed. A release of will to whim is an action whose movements are part of the future, not merely oriented towards the future: they command the future. Sense apprehension divines a place for action, for new possibilities that seem to open up in desirable directions. Complete involvement in the arch-movement, unrestricted by the shame of hatred, dictates the substance of becoming.

"The greatest theory in use" proposes that affective discernment can instruct ethical action. A scrupulous apprehension of circumstances allows for ethical living as activism:

> Without any shadow of doubt, amidst this vertigo of shows and politics, I settle myself ever the firmer in the creed that we should not postpone and refer and wish, but do broad justice where we are, by whomsoever we deal with, accepting our actual companions and circumstances, however humble or odious, as the mystic officials to whom the universe has delegated its whole pleasure for us (W 3:60).

Emerson's point is that redemption is not in the afterlife but in the here and now. Our participation in negotiating justice is as much a "Beautiful Necessity" as the acceptance of fate.

This sort of acquiescence does not imply free-ranging whimsicality. As Nietzsche argues in *Twilight*, learning to see requires a "hostile calm" ("Germans" 6) to obviate a reactionary instinct. The complete subjectivity of the thinking body actively inspects a stimulus rather than categorizing like-stimuli; it takes its remove from an influx of light in order to see clearly. This active way of seeing prizes the object, but is unlike the "modern objectivity" that Nietzsche criticizes as "bad taste" (ibid.) in its cold and passive apprehension. This kind of spying on reality does not take itself into account, which is the necessary condition for an aesthetic mode of observation: "To see what is… one must know who one is" ("Skirmishes" 7). Learning to see requires "a suspension of the will" ("Germans" 6) and we are to understand that this suspension is unreasonable, emotive, and irrational, acting as a kind of self-subversion. For both Nietzsche and Emerson, the intense egoism of the naysayer was a necessary heroism: critical thinking enables ethical action by the implication of its actor.

Emerson as Educator

"Schopenhauer as Educator" was a work that was close to Nietzsche's heart. He had sent a copy of it to Lou Von Salomé, attesting that its contents crystallized his philosophy. In the essay, Nietzsche does not account for Schopenhauer's philosophy, rather, he traces his own foundational passions. Emerson is twice cited, both references to his essay "Circles". Why not entitle the work "Emerson as Educator"? Apart from Nietzsche's tendency to keep Emerson's presence silent, Schopenhauer offered something that Emerson could not: the negativity necessary for change. But Schopenhauer's world-view was not Dionysian. Nietzsche's understanding of the Dionysian was outlined in the dialectical framework of his earlier work, *The Birth of Tragedy*. Kaufmann pointed out that Nietzsche abandoned this dialectical view after the publication of *The Birth of Tragedy*, on the way to formulating a monadological pluralism.[129] Perhaps we can understand Emerson's influence as a provocation against the dualistic view, taking into account "Schopenhauer as Educator" as a work that expounds on "Circles" throughout.

We can hear Emerson's presence in "Schopenhauer" from the start, where Nietzsche argues that one must be oneself above all,36 but his two direct references occur at the end of the essay, indicating rhetorically that they are summative of ideas expressed within it. The first reference is unattributed: "Who was it who said the true word—'A man has never risen higher than when he knoweth not whither his road may yet lead him'?" (1) Nietzsche's framing of the citation, which is attributed in "Circles" to Oliver Cromwell, occurs a few lines earlier: "There is in the world only one way, on which nobody can go, except you: where does it lead? Do not ask, go along with it" (1). In the context of Emerson's essay, the Cromwell quotation is preceded by these lines:

---

129   Kaufmann, *Nietzsche*, 156.

> The one thing which we seek with insatiable desire is to forget ourselves, to be surprised out of our propriety, to lose our semipiternal memory and to do something without knowing how or why; in short to draw a new circle. Nothing great was ever achieved without enthusiasm. The way of life is wonderful. It is by abandonment (321).

In Nietzsche's reading, he underlined "The one thing which we seek with insatiable desire is to forget ourselves;" "to draw a new circle;" "wonderful;" and "by abandonment". In the next paragraph, he traced seven vertical lines next to the Cromwell quote; and one long vertical line and two short alongside the last two sentences.38 The excitement expressed by the marks indicate that Nietzsche was moved by these lines. The four sentences in Emerson's paragraph express the foundational principles of *amor fati*. Self-overcoming, willingness, the end of shame, will to power, and the affirmation of the natural choreography of impulse constitute Nietzsche's "formula for greatness," whose basic principle is that we must affirm here to get to there with a detachment from the herd instinct and all its normative modes of getting-there.

The second citation of Emerson, the one that Nietzsche attributes to him, emphasizes the revolutionary "thinker" as the agent or event that informs a paradigm shift: "'Beware when the great God lets loose a thinker on this planet,' says Emerson, "Then all things are at risk'" (p. 308). Uncharacteristically, Nietzsche cited the entire passage, emphasizing the dangers of such change. The word "conflagration" was used to refer to the death of God. Although the void itself was not perceived as dangerous—as Emerson wrote: "Blessed be nothing!" (W 2:315)—the destruction of the old eradicates the meaning of much of its cultural artifacts, so that all meaning is in peril. Whatever is universal in the cultural mechanism survives.

What is universal are the "hieroglyphics of human life" (4) that emphasize Nietzsche's unattributed quotations of Emerson, summoning his phrase "every man's condition is a solution in hieroglyphic to those inquiries he would put" (*Nature*):

> Who are they that will lift us? They are those true men, those who are no longer animal, the *philosophers, artists, and saints*. Nature, which never makes a leap, made its one leap in creating

them, and a leap of joy moreover, for nature then feels that for the first time, it has reached its goal—where it realizes that it has to unlearn having goals and that it has played the game of life and becoming at too high stakes (5).

Nietzsche's emphasis, in his original italics, persists a few paragraphs later in the same section:

> It is the fundamental idea of culture, insofar as it sets in each of us but one task: to promote the production of the *philosopher, the artist and the saint* within us and without us and thereby to work at the perfection of nature. For as nature needs the philosopher, so does it need the artist, for the achievement of a metaphysical goal (5).

The unattributed references are to lines in Emerson's essay "History," which serve as the epigraph to *The Gay Science*: "To the poet, to the philosopher, to the saint, all things are friendly and sacred" (13). Nietzsche substituted "the poet" for "the artist," indicating his preference for Goethe's term that affirms the dramatic poet as the essential revolutionary. This makes sense: as a type of activism, drama is an illusion that affirms being over becoming. If the play's the thing, the moment of transfiguration is enlightenment. To initiate this sort of enlightenment, Nietzsche proposes a "new circle of duties". The phrase, "Kreis von Pflichten," is repeated four times in section five.

The aim of the "new circle of duties" was to educate humankind to live beyond animality by virtue of a vision of humanity "as something that stands high above us" (5). Nietzsche wrote that there are moments when we become aware of our "real metaphysical significance" by the apprehension of "a profound feeling of oneness and identity with all living things" (5). But we need someone to uplift us, to lead us away from the "false philosopher" who "'without hope lives in desire," and for whom beauty does not animate "the petrified doctrine of 'becoming'" (5). It is clear that the "philosophical genius" proposed at the end of the essay was not Schopenhauer. It was Emerson.

Circles

Of all of Emerson's works, arguably the most philosophical is his essay "Circles," which nonetheless proclaims resistance to philosophical, religious and scientific dogma. In its aspiration towards the future, Emerson's truth is not absolute but experiential: the heart contains it. New ideas replace the old. Nothing is settled; everything is process and predilection. We can know nothing certainly. There is only feeling, action, and the attraction of words.

In Emerson's vision, there is no stable "I," because everything is always moving. The "I"—or the eye as "the first circle"— is a matter of geometry. It changes according to the circumference of a circle; its radius is always shifting. Subjectivity is what expounds from the circle's center. Actions that effect change create new circles. One who is capable of creating a new circle prefers the truth of the moment to "his past apprehension of truth" (p. 309). A longing for freedom and a "quick and strong" (p. 309) soul comprise the power it takes to make a new circle.

For Emerson, thought is a cause that is an effect of "a finer cause," (p. 305) suggesting that cause and effect are of the same nature. He does not name the ultimate cause. Rhetorically, he indicates that he is not convinced of its identity:

> Nature looks provokingly stable and secular, but it has a cause like all the rest; and when once I comprehend that, will these fields stretch so immovably wide, these leaves hang so individually considerable?" (p. 303).

His hedging expresses uncertainty. For lack of a better term, he names the initial cause "Being," which stands at the center of the circle and is the means by which becoming is made sensible. Being is "superior to creation, superior to knowledge and thought, and contains all its circles," (p. 318) but it does not delimit "eternal procession" (p. 314) regarding the creative action of the human mind. The "eternal generator" ceaselessly generates with an aim to forge "a life and thought as large and excellent as itself" (p. 318). Like a benevolent parent, it recognizes "that which is made instructs how to make a better" (318). In other words, "Being" evolves and is compatible with self-determination.

Though Emerson cites scripture in "Circles," referring to the Gospel of Paul, he rejects the metaphysical Jesus in his journal, preferring a physical consecration of the divine (8:227-28). He describes Jesus and Berkeley each as a "crude statement of the fact that all nature is the rapid efflux of goodness executing and organizing itself" (p. 310). He admits that even his privileging of the moral sentiment is a sensibility:

> I own I am gladdened by seeing the predominance of the saccharine principle throughout vegetable nature, and not less by beholding in morals that unrestrained inundation of the principle of good into every chink and hole that selfishness has left open, yea into selfishness and sin itself; so that no evil is pure, nor hell itself without its extreme satisfactions (p. 318).

Like Nietzsche's "ideal of a superhuman well-being and benevolence," Emerson's vision of an absolute good that interpenetrates nature presents a philosophy of "the dangerous Perhaps" (BGE 2).

To the charge that the philosopher will build temples on the virtue of circles, Emerson's unassailable response is "I am only an experimenter, with no Past at my back." (p. 318) Nietzsche paid attention to this in his reading; he underlined it and in the margins alongside wrote "Ja??" The question is charged positively in Nietzsche's rhetoric, suggesting how much the idea of experimental philosophy meant to him. It is the foundational question that he addresses in *Beyond Good and Evil* as a new mode of philosophy:

> A new sort of philosopher is emerging: I venture to baptize them with a name which is not without danger. As I figure them out - to the extent that they let themselves be figured out, for it belongs to their type to want to remain something of an enigma - these philosophers of the future may have a right, perhaps also a wrong, to be described as attempters. This name itself is finally merely an attempt and, if you will, a temptation (42).

The triple meanings of the German root *Versuch* translate as experiment, attempt, and temptation. We observe the growing metaphor related to Emerson: the dangerous temptation conjures the riddle of the Sphinx.

In "Circles," we understand that "our life is an apprenticeship to the truth" that is chronically mediated; the truth itself is "unattainable, the flying perfect" (p. 301). "Our moods do not believe in each other" but "every man believes he has a greater possibility" (p. 306) towards which he is guided by his instincts. Accessing this possibility requires enthusiasm and self-abandonment: enthusiasm initiates; abandonment succeeds. Overcoming the negative requires some sort of reception. Emerson specifically defines reception as poetic illumination that provides the distance that we need to see our situations. Literature provides "a purchase by which we may move" (p. 312) our present life. We receive ourselves in the accounts of others. Our reading gives us the power to break through the dimensions of the present moment and access another time.

Eternal Procession

In the fragments of *Will to Power*, Nietzsche described eternal recurrence as a "great cultivating idea" whose aim was to employ "the selective principle in the service of strength" (1053). Emerson described a similar principle in "Circles": "The same law that we call eternal procession ranges all that we call the virtues, and extinguishes each in the light of a better" (p. 314). Emerson's procession entails the evolutionary improvement of the value of what is good; Nietzsche's recurrence involves evolutionary improvement in the creation of the Overman.

Both writers committed to an anthropocentric view early in their careers, but later distanced themselves from it. Emerson's man-centered vision in nature transformed in "Experience" to universal "Being," whose nature is impersonal. He elaborated on this in his later collection, *The Conduct of Life*, principally in the essays "Fate" and "Circles," where "Being" presents as a cosmological physics. Likewise, Nietzsche's early *Untimely Meditations* focused on human drives, but his will to power in later works, specifically in *Beyond Good and Evil*, proposes what Paul Loeb called "Power Physics," which he defines as the subatomic drive to dominance in a hierarchical cosmology.[130]

The will to power in the form of *amor fati*, however, suggests that the drive is not to dominate but to affirm the complex. In *Beyond Good and Evil*, Nietzsche wrote that the purely solipsistic will cannot act on itself (36); the singular will to power is part of the will to power of the whole, which he frames in The *Will to Power* as "pathos," (635) an impersonal force that is influenced by ethos. This reasoning is a development of an earlier aphorism (WP 490) where Nietzsche posited the pluralized "I" as an "aristocracy of equals, who are accustomed to ruling cooperatively," qualifying the will to power as not simply a tyrannical drive.[131] Eternal recurrence becomes a symbiotic orientation to change in a hierarchy whose authority persistently shifts.

Emerson's reasoning around "eternal procession" is remarkably similar to the ideas that ground Nietzsche's eternal recurrence.[132] Outside of time, the energy that ceaselessly generates informs a process that negates agency, spiritualizes thought and institutes human faith as the material for the construction of an ethical system that is not unlike Christianity. "Eternal procession" might be a more accurate term for what Nietzsche meant by eternal recurrence.   The circle within the circle is an image of eternal recurrence, whereas the spiral seems to be the image of eternal procession: a line follows the circular curve but does not meet itself. Recurrence of the same delimits the new, closing the circle rather opening it in the continuity of a spiral. Considering the "eternal" aspect, however, in the logic of moments—

130   Paul S. Loeb, "Will to Power and Panpsychism: A New Exegesis of BGE 36" in Nietzsche on Mind and Nature, ed. Manuel Dries and P.J.E. Kail (Oxford:Oxford University Press, 2015).

131   The reasoning is also corroborated later in WP: ""Everything organic, that 'judges,' acts like the artist: it creates stimuli into a whole from individual suggestions, it leaves many things aside and creates a simplification, it equates and affirms its creature as being. The logical is the drive itself, which makes the world run according to our judgment. " Nachlass 1884 25[333], (KSA 11:97).

132   Fabricus translated eternal progression here as "ewigen Fortganges." But Nietzsche's original eternal return was expressed either as "ewigen wiederkunft" or "ewigen wiederkehr." The term "Wiederkunft" is used to describe the Second Coming as in "die Wiederkunft Christi [auf Erden]."

following Emerson's idea of time in "History" where the multidimensional here and now compacts the past, the present, and the future, like spacetime—the circle is a better metaphor than the spiral to describe discrete moments whose area is what Deleuze calls "the transcendental field".[133] Still, Emerson's spiral-like procession entails invention in its wiry line rather than the complacency of return. This configurational conflict is represented in physics by the wave versus particle dynamic. Perhaps it is both.

---

133   Deleuze, The Logic of Sense, trans. Mark Lester (New York: Columbia University Press, 1993), 97-98.

Part V.

WOMAN

Hermeneutics of Woman

Nietzsche's complex attitude towards woman, like his attitude towards benevolence, changes over the course of his writing. In his early works, she is presented as a divine object, associated with music and the assimilation of the strange. This association is cultivated in *The Gay Science* in the production of artistic woman who, like all of her gender, wishes to be possessed. Nietzsche mostly keeps his distance from woman in *Thus Spake Zarathustra*, where she is "the most dangerous plaything" ("Woman" 18) whose sole purpose is the propagation of the Overman. But in *Beyond Good and Evil*, where woman is the symbol for virtue and truth, he gets in her face. His provocation was deliberate: he meant to extirpate woman along with virtue and in order to do so, he attacked both. This challenge to the values of woman and virtue only increase their significance. The sacred woman resurfaces in *Ecce Homo* by way of Nietzsche's recursion to the "genius of the heart." His cycling of woman becomes an eternal return to Ariadne. The sacred woman was Nietzsche's persistent ideal.

The function of Nietzsche's attacks on woman are manifold: conceptually, woman always stands in the way of his self-overcoming. This woman is like the Sphinx whose riddle must be answered. In the Dionysian frame, woman is Ariadne, his "ear" that hears a tentative affirmation of life. Poetically, she is Baubo the bawd, a monstrous consolation, perhaps a version of himself. Metaphorically, woman as life must be loved; woman as music must be played; woman as virtue must be eradicated. Finally, there is woman as she presents herself, "woman as she is," e.g. George Eliot, George Sand or Germaine De Staël. She is the enemy, whom Nietzsche must engage. It is his nature: he is a warrior and both life and love are war.

Rhetorically, she is all the same. There is only one woman who presents as the symbolic aspect of Nietzsche's reckoning. This rhetorical woman acts as his woman-as-she-is and woman-as-I-am, the alien other that he struggles with in his process of writing. She appears in Sphinx form as a ferocious provocation whose riddle exposes Nietzsche's essential passion. This internal, symbolic woman, who contained the clash of willingness and will, is first the object of Nietzsche's cruelty, because "in all desire to know there is already a drop of cruelty," (BGE 230) and then becomes the subject of *amor fati* wherein willingness replaces will.

Sacred Women

Nietzsche's struggle against woman ends in the embrace of a passive position: *I am that*, creating an ambiguity as nebulous as the *vita femina*. Woman is already, following the destiny of anatomy, a plurality. It is precisely this maternal figure that Nietzsche esteems in his discussion of Plato's *Republic*. In his early essay, "The Greek Woman," both the female Guardian, whose excellence grants her the right to procreation, and the priestess at Delphi, the Pythian ear of Apollo, are sacred objects deprived of subjectivity for the sake of the state. Nietzsche implies that the Guardian mothers and the Oracle willed themselves as objects in order to seduce even Plato to succumb to their divining instincts. As he winks at the end of the essay, their particular virtue—prescience—was the kind of affinity with nature that made them superior to men. His philosophy sought to assume the position of such excellence even as he degraded the actual female.

If the declaration of *amor fati* was his coded assent to the feminine, how did Nietzsche embrace the "secondary role" (BGE 145) of the female, the passive position in the dynamics of power? What does *amor fati* have to do with sublimation of the female, or more precisely, what does woman have to do with the will to power? In The *Will to Power*, he wrote:

> Woman! One-half of mankind is weak, typically sick, change-able, inconstant... she needs a religion of weakness that glorifies being weak, loving, and being humble as divine: or better, she makes the strong weak—she rules when she succeeds in overcoming the strong... Woman has always conspired with the types of decadence, the priests, against the 'powerful', the 'strong', the men- (864).

His position is consistent with his established anti-woman stance, but it is inconsistent with the condition of *amor fati*, which is pregnant with the female and paralyzed by humility. This female figure accepts everything as necessary and will "not only bear it but love it," (EH "Books" 10) affirming the "the logic and illogicality of entanglements" (WP 1041) as "the highest condition a philosopher can reach". As "wisdom and love for wisdom," (KSA 11:145) *amor fati* is the coming philosophy, acting as the fallen ideal to which dogmatic philosophers have strived but none has won.

Nietzsche's general misogyny can be understood as a sublimation of the female for the sake of the will to power, which involves the amelioration of the human race. This sublimation purports truth to be ephemeral, like the "dangerous and beautiful cat" (BGE 239) that presents itself in rare moments to make life worth living. The truth and the woman, though rarely revealed, are omnipresent.

The Gay Science

Emerson's orientation to the female was patriarchal whereas Nietzsche was plainly misogynistic. His most energetic bursts of woman-hate occur in his later works, *Beyond Good and Evil* and *Ecce Homo*, intensified from his earlier work, *The Gay Science*, where his contempt for women takes the form of condescension. Nietzsche invites "women and their action at a distance" only after making the claim that artists and lovers associate their disgust for nature with a disgust for women, which is inseparable from their love for women. But the magical women who appear in the aphorism elicit the confession from the man who regards them that "he almost believes that his better self resides there amongst" them. In the larger context, we assume that Nietzsche believed his better self was actually the silent wanderer exalted in the previous aphorism, *We Artists*, whose project to conceal nature effectively concealed women.

In Book One of *The Gay Science*, Nietzsche identifies as an artist rather than a philosopher (59), a switch in roles that is justified in his revision by the claim that past philosophers had ignored the spirit of music, meaning that they disregarded life out of fear of its seductions, namely, those of the sirens, and in so doing dismissed the feminine entirely as a way to understand it (372). His introduction of Dionysian pessimism in the second edition proposed to dispose this bloodless apprehension of life in favor of a creative philosophy forged from the

spirit of love rather than revenge (370). His association of woman
with music, and musical woman with learning describes a psychological process that effectively countered Schopenhauer's influence—his
abnegation of feeling and rabid misogyny—at once as it sublimated
woman in Nietzsche's aesthetics.

As an artist, Nietzsche can hear "the woman in music," (63)
evoking a sense of the sacred carried by the wind that seems to lead
him where he should go against his will. But he prefers not to listen:
the female voice cannot be trusted. His encoded reference to Emerson's "fair girl" in "Women... at a distance" considers direct advocacy
for women, and rejects it as noise.

In *The Gay Science*, Nietzsche's woman is in a constant state
of exclusion owing to her bad reputation, which he claims is more
difficult to control than bad conscience: "what things are called is un-
speakably more important than what they are" (52), a notion that illus-
trates his valuation of surfaces in the book at large. Bringing style to
one's character requires the formulation of appearances in "an artistic
plan," so that people are "bound by but also perfected under their own
law" (290). Nietzsche wrote that this stylization is for strong characters; the weak-minded (with whom he seemed to identify) prefer the
appearance of accident. In either case, the aim is self-determination
gained through creative expression. Becoming what one is starts with
the cultivation of appearances; it starts with language. Without words,
Nietzsche's woman is an *homo sacer*: her life is insignificant as that of a
heifer.

But it seems that Nietzsche's hidden intention was to instruct
women. An elaboration of his pedagogical position occurs in "Will
and Willingness" (68). The wise man in the aphorism says that "men
corrupt women," and that "the way of man is will; the way of woman
is willingness" (68). The "youth," however, the "one in the company"
whom we might take as representing Nietzsche, believes that educating
women, not men, to overcome the corruption imposed by men is the
way to overcome it. While the wise man advises teaching men not to
corrupt women, the youth's solution is to teach women in a cruel way
to become more willful. This moment suggests that Nietzsche's stance
towards woman was an intentional provocation meant to teach her
about the dismal attitudes that constitute common misogyny, to train
her warrior instincts and justify her to herself.

At the end of the first edition of *The Gay Science*, Nietzsche's *vita femina* lifts the veil of becoming. This glimpse of life as a woman acts as a principle vision whose rarity comprises its value. Life as a woman is "the strongest magic," presenting illusions of "beautiful possibilities, woven with threads of gold - promising, resisting, bashful, mocking, compassionate, and seductive" (339). The woman herself does not redeem; rather Nietzsche implicates an exotic, feminine beauty. But by the end of the second edition, the justification of life as an enchanting woman is reframed around the notion that life is a woman whom we accept but now doubt.

We might understand Nietzsche's revisions to the second edition as a re-approach to the problem of woman in part because his new preface was dedicated to one: the prankster goddess Baubo. In his preface, "truth is a woman;" in Book One, woman is potentially dangerous; in Book Two, she is kept at a distance; in Book Three, she has the potential for greatness; in Book Four, life is a woman; and in Book Five, Nietzsche becomes a woman, exposing himself by redressing "The problem of the actor". The actor is acknowledged as an artist, which means that Nietzsche was also an actor, aligning him with the women who "try to be 'taken for something' even as they are being taken" (361). The question of whether his revision indicates that Nietzsche, having identified with woman, wanted to be loved as he claimed a woman wants to be loved—i.e., taken as an object—is answered at the end of Book Five when he hears his prior works groaning at him, becoming demanding objects independent of his will.

Beyond Good and Evil

In *Beyond Good and Evil*, Nietzsche's woman performs as a rhetorical figure that processes emotional resistance in the development of his thought. He extracts woman along with virtue: she is no longer "coiled within the labyrinth of an ear".[134] The slights against her are not mere undertones, intended for the initiated. She is visible on the stage, though not quite whole. His animosity erupts as vitriol throughout the "Our Virtues" section. Did his intensity of feeling be-

---

134   Derrida, *Spurs*, 43.

lie concern for woman? Judging by what he wrote and how he wrote it, his position does not seem feigned. He sounds like an authentic misogynist. Despite himself, he praises woman, whose "ineducability and inner savagery" (231) indicate that she is superior to men. By the established connection of woman with what is good—the feminine moment that redeems in nature, music and learning— Nietzsche's affirmation of himself as woman presents as the complicated affirmation of his own virtue.

Nietzsche's disposition to the female in "the genius of the heart" passage expresses a transparent declaration of love for Ariadne, who can be understood as a symbol for the narrative thread in writing wherein the writer is charged with seeking himself in the labyrinth. In the process of writing, Nietzsche could not avoid the Sphinx, the rhetorical woman tied up in writing as a mode of thinking, feeling and learning. The frightening specter repeatedly interrupts his excavation of virtue (214). As he bravely approached moments of revelation, he encountered the Sphinx, was threatened by her supernatural savagery and promptly defended himself by launching attacks. Every instance of woman hate occurs when Nietzsche was reckoning with new ideas.

Writing is the medium in which conscience is expressed. Nietzsche's attitude towards conscience is stated in the beginning of "Our Virtues," where he confronted the problem of belief, which is a problem because of its association with the morality that he intended to purge. Beliefs are tried in conscientious thinking wherein the question of what is beneficial is addressed. Our serviceable virtues, as Nietzsche saw them, should be self-interested. They should be "those only which have come to agreement with our most secret and heartfelt inclinations, with our most ardent requirement" (214). These "inclinations" and "requirements" are defined in the next two aphorisms: we desire variety; we need enemies (215-16). In order to love better, we need to hate more. This connection between love and hate is the vital junction between Nietzsche and woman; it is where Nietzsche meets woman as her instructor in the art of war. His hate-speech regarding women becomes intentional provocation. Her chastity—her unwillingness to engage—is her final vice.

Nietzsche's performance in *Beyond Good and Evil* dramatizes classic misogynistic prejudices. He launches a series of attacks on woman, starting with "the clever ones," (231) including De Staël, whom he advised to be silent in politics. De Staël is targeted again as "comical," (233) expressing the prejudice that seriousness in social commentary should be limited to men. Woman as nurturer is likewise debased: the female cannot cook well; her most esteemed acts of care are to grant the male his license to pleasure. Her gravest efforts ought to be loving her man and looking good (235). Nietzsche exhorts his readers to regard women as the "Orientals" (235) do: by strict possession of them, according to logic that a man's love for a woman is the desire to possess her (GS 363). This attitude continues in the last aphorism of "Our Virtues" that assails the disenchantment of women. "Free spirits and literary workers," such as De Staël and Sand, are threats to the power of woman, whose "unattainableness and innate wildness" (239) consecrate her power over men. In Nietzsche's scheme, woman's Apollonian ascent effects her Dionysian desecration: if she is no longer a force of nature, and if there is "no God concealed beneath" her, there is nothing for mankind but "a modern idea" (239).

Mankind, Nietzsche asserts, is disposed with a combination of "fear and sympathy" (239) for woman. But the sympathy is troublesome: it arrives with contempt. Nietzsche blames woman, who is "clairvoyant in the art of suffering," (239) for placing sympathy in the hands of poets. Sympathy is confused with love, and love with the desire to die, thanks, of course, to woman. This is where the teaching of the "genius of the heart" became germane to Nietzsche's regard of the other. The genius teaches love that is not sentimental, love that is "more uncertain perhaps, more tender, more fragile, more broken, but full of hopes which as yet have no names, full of new will and flowing" (295). Love is clearly defined as war, but in the "genius" sections, love seeks strength, profundity and beauty by way of a feminized power. Sympathy in the frame of this idiosyncratic love is an expression of cowardice that attempts to sanctify itself. Cruelty is prescribed.

Nietzsche's attempts to educate women account for his inclination to attack them. The purpose of education, as he states in "Schopenhauer as Educator," is to understand "what the real raw material of your being is, something quite uneducable, yet in any case accessible only with difficulty, bound, paralyzed: your educators can be only your liberators" (I). It seems plain that the purpose of his provocation of women was to lead her back to nature, away from the acculturation that would threaten her natural power. His basic argument was that woman must remain profane in order to preserve her sacred status. Her debasement allows the ascension of Ariadne, who is polarized by the chthonic Circe, whom we cannot trust. As an ideal, woman represents the possibility for female power only if she, like the eternal feminine, affirms man. Woman's power—her feral will—remains subterranean in Nietzsche's scheme, a position that justifies violence against her.

Ecce Homo

Nietzsche instigates a similar processing of woman through equivocal language in the transparent opacity of *Ecce Homo*. Like Heraclitus, he distanced himself from the words he wrote: his first line in "Why I Write Such Excellent Books" is "I am one and my words another." This statement prefaces his explanation of himself regarding the concerns of his published works, in which he abruptly insists that he knows woman. He refers to the "genius of the heart" section to describe the nature of his psychology. The reference presents an allusion to Ariadne even as it forewords another misogynistic fit, similar to the succession of anti-woman aphorisms in the end of "Our Virtues". The same pattern ensues: his logic implodes and from this destruction, woman appears.

Nietzsche spells out his devotion to women in *Beyond Good and Evil*, declaring that he loves best when he despises most (216). This dismissal of disinterest in love qualifies his claim in *Ecce Homo* that women only appreciate egoistic men, suggesting that his performance of egoism in the book was an attempt to charm them. He describes his ideal readers in "Why I Write Such Excellent Books," stating pointedly that feminists are excluded. Feminism is understood as a kind of "malicious 'idealism'" (3) meant to destroy sexual love, practiced by barren, vengeful women. In his reasoning, the most womanly woman "fights tooth and nail against rights in general" because "the natural order of things, the eternal war between the sexes, assigns to her by far the foremost rank" (5). Among these womanly women are the "aimiable Maenads," Dionysian lovers who "tear you to pieces" (5). These women resemble the Sphinx.

Considering Nietzsche's conflation of hate with love, we have to ask whether his animosity towards feminism was an expression of devotion towards feminists, cloaked in the rhetoric of opposition. We wonder whether his ideal reader was the "little woman" he described in the section, who, "pursuing her vengeance, would force open even the iron gates of Fate itself" (5)? She seems to be related to the "bewitched little woman" listed among the "Great men" in *The Gay Science*. Is this woman, who combines the political interests of "woman-as-such" with the metaphysical powers of the Sphinx, also actually a feminist, whom Nietzsche meant to provoke by her exclusion? He states plainly in the 'Why I Am So Wise" section that "attacking is proof of good will," (7) suggesting that we are to take his misogyny as proof of his benevolence towards woman. If his provocations were meant to spur woman towards her "liberation" by way of war against men in the condition of "an honorable duel," (7) then his vehement disparagement of political women was a tacit affirmation of feminism.

Nietzsche's appraisal of surfaces, however, points to a literal interpretation of his hatred for "woman as such". Though we understand that this hatred also expresses love, it is not enough to undo the damage that his writing substantiates. As Nietzsche wrote in *The Gay Science*, "What others know (or think they know) about us assails us" (52). Bad reputation cannot be easily overcome, least of all in ourselves. Conceptualizing Derrida's "ear of the other," or the ear as labyrinth, the female reader of Nietzsche is presented with her own labyrinth. She must solve herself to herself, following the thread, taking the word as a way to affirm her own power. She must write herself, confronting the Sphinx.

The Feminine Operation

In *Eperons: le Style de Nietzsche*, Derrida proposes that Nietzsche's woman was composed in the process of writing, emerging as a kind of style that illuminates the problem of possession and loss, as in the famous loss of Nietzsche's umbrella as it corresponds to the absence of "the style, the simulacrum, the woman".[135] Nietzsche's writing implies that, in Derrida's words, "if there is going to be style,

---

135   Derrida, Spurs, 139.

there can only be more than one". But, as Nietzsche insisted in *Ecce Homo*, his style was deliberate. His provocations were calibrated to his reader's ear; he took pains to express his ideas with brutal concision, "with cold but roguish hostility towards all 'beautiful words' and 'beautiful feelings'" ("Books" 5). He cultivated this type of writing—"condense, severe" ("Books" 5)—as the medium for a message that indirectly reveals his version of truth. The woman in Nietzsche's writing is not style but *bios*, Agamben's political life, an avid constituent in the mediation of woman, though not a woman herself.

The incorporation of the other in not a problem with writing—it is writing—but with reading. The umbrella statement remains enigmatic. Our powerlessness to apprehend its meaning invalidates any attempt at decoding it. We cannot know. But, as Derrida explained, the attempt of reading is to "perforate...the hermeneutic sail," to discover "its what for, or why, like a woman or like writing, it passes itself off for what it passes itself off for".[136] In other words, we can try to understand the protocol of the text itself. What does the text want? Derrida infers that the text wants protection: it will not get wet from the insidious Heraclitan moisture associated with women.

In Derrida's dalliance with the woman of Nietzsche's text, the spur digs deeper in her. He produces perplexing sentences, like this:

> If it is necessary to keep one's distance from the feminine operation, from the *actio in distans* (to mistake this necessity for just another "approach" however would be to risk death itself), it is perhaps because the "woman" is not a determinable identity.[137]

Earlier, he defines "the feminine operation" as Nietzsche's inscription of truth, feminine because it is indiscernible. His logic follows that if truth is female, then "style must return to her".[138] Derrida teases a feminist approach regarding Nietzsche's rare praise of women—"Must not these apparently feminist propositions be reconciled with the

136   Ibid., 127.

137   Ibid., 57.

138   Ibid.

overwhelming corpus of Nietzsche's vehement anti-feminism?"—and then demurs: "Their congruence (a notion which I oppose by convention to that of appearance), although ineluctably enigmatic, is just as rigorously necessary".[139]   In his reasoning, to re-approach the contradiction, which he prefers to imagine as "congruence," between Nietzsche's implied feminism and his outright misogyny, is to violate appearances.   In short, "woman" needs the "veil" or she will not be "desirable".[140]   Nietzsche's woman is cursed by this mystification and its accompanying mistrust. Rather than confront this curse with his own affirmations or negations, Derrida enshrouds her in the veil of his own discourse. His undressing and redressing her does little more than perform as intrigue.

Gayatri Spivak, in her essay-blog on *Eperons*, reminds us that deconstruction is affirmation of the text.[141]   By playing along with Nietzsche's hermeneutics, never quite exposing them, Derrida engrosses the metaphor of woman. He takes the same abused object and submerges her deeper in the romantic imagination. We see Nietzsche there aside woman, wishing he had not forgotten his umbrella.

With Nietzsche and Derrida, we see the sacrifice of woman on the surface for the sake of her eternal mysteries, the sanctification of the woman object as a hermeneutical position in writing.   When he writes "elle s'écrit,"[142] Derrida makes no claim to explicit meaning. "Elle s'écrit" is not much different from Nietzsche's "Non legor, non legar" (EH "Books" 1). In each case, the inscrutability of the subject, first woman then Nietzsche, is emphasized. The irony is of course that man has written woman, rather than woman writing herself. Nietzsche wrote woman, literally, and deliberately developed her romantic potential at the expense of her actuality. His "I am not read, I will not be read" is a similar deliberate mystification of himself. In each case, with Nietzsche and with woman, the possibilities for interpreta-

---

139   Ibid.

140   Ibid., 59.

141   Gayatri Spivak, "Displacement and the Discourse of Woman" in Displacement: Derrida and After, Mark Krupnik, ed. (Bloomington: Indiana UP, 1983), 169-95.

142   Derrida, Spurs, 43-44.

tion are increased. To be read means to be interpreted wholly, to be held in the text. To be written means to be othered from oneself; it also means to be formed. Ironically, she does not form herself; he does.

Derrida's ascription of Nietzsche's style as woman is similar to Jung's description of the finer part of man's soul as anima. Both assumed the position of the male negotiating a female sensibility inherent in the male psyche, but this does not work for a female writer. First, if writing is *difference*, a female writer's cultivation of anima as style is not produced in sexual difference and is therefore taken as less fecund. The female writer's appropriation of animus is likewise ineffective: she becomes the sort of feminist that Derrida derides as a soulless bureaucrat.[143] This normative approach further distances the gender-fluid writer from the assumption of style's dynamics. The position of the male poetic thinker in Jung and Derrida appropriates the female as anima as it actively disdains the actual female.

Deconstructionism is feminization, as Spivak wrote.[144] It is also solipsistic. Man affirms himself via his claim to the internal language of a text. Woman is never identical to herself. She is affirmed as the object, which in the Gorgian sense of solipsism—if the subject is the object—implies a deferred subjectivity. Through woman, man affirms himself; through man, woman is affirmed. How are we to account for the passive: she is affirmed? Nature moves, and is moved. It moves her; she is moved by nature, by her nature, which as Spivak reiterated, is never the same as itself.[145] To say that woman has no identity with herself is to say she has no integrity. As an object ever beyond herself, she has no powers of mediation. She is run by men.

In other words, woman in the history of philosophy has been wrought in rhetoric, and as such, is ever untrue. She is associated with falsehood by Spivak, who elaborates Derrida's interpretation of Nietzsche's "woman 'give themselves' even when they give themselves" as false orgasm—faked power, faked pleasure— that directs meaning-making, permitting feminized freedom in the art of writing.[146]

---

143   Ibid., 65.

144   Spivak, Displacement, 173.

145   Ibid.

146   Ibid., 44.

Woman is thus rendered in illusion; she becomes illusion. Her giving of herself implies that she wills herself as the object. If anatomy is destiny, then maleness is the performance of subjectivity: the male writer sanctifies himself with the military strength of sentence-making as command. As Spivak wrote, he must perform as he cannot bluff the act.[147] Femaleness is the reception of such subjectivity: she is the space for the other. As such, she is not for herself.

Unanswerable Dictations

Like the language of existentialism that Theodor Adorno criticized in *The Jargon of Authenticity*, the jargon of deconstruction has become an institution. The problem with terms like "*difference*," "displacement" and "residue" is that they have become parts of a system whose approach to meaning, as generative textual capaciousness in the emptiness of the female space, has strangled itself. Though we have a new tool with this approach, a feminized tool notwithstanding its male construction, its excessive insistence on inquiry is a performance of the magistery of its author. The specialness of meaning-making is left to the uber-professionals, the self-appointed disciples of Athena who prescribe a meaning within the jargon.

The text, in fact, does not stand alone. Its writing is not a solipsistic action, but a collaborative action, available to the reader in the coding of allusion. Reading is also not a solipsistic action. Interpretations always go beyond a text, not just to the reader, but to other texts in which they are seeded. The text itself does not generate; rather, the reader whose connection to the other texts is the generative force. The idea of pure meaningfulness that deconstruction ascribes—meaning in and for itself—disregards the thriving associations among texts in its attempt to divine language as an ideal. "Residue" and "displacement" direct us towards unanswerable dictations whose ambiguous resolutions are oblivious to the obvious questions "from whence?" and "of what?" in order, it seems, to exoticize origins and position a metaphysics of meaning-in-itself within the solipsistic associations of its supervisor. Actual traces, residue and displacement refer outside

147   Ibid.

the text. This is where the reader finds herself, dissatisfied with the impervious affirmations of Nietzsche's sacred/profane woman. If woman is taken as sacred, she is no longer real, and as such cannot advance the benefit of her actual power in the political realm, where she is sorely needed.

It seems that Nietzsche did not know women, as he claimed, but he did love them—if it is possible to love and not to know—as he sought to prepare them for the strong Apollonian light. It might have been simpler for him to advocate for women, as Emerson did.[148] Instead, they are the sacred animal, never quite possessed, always more than one, never not detestable, with the exception of Ariadne, who has suffered at length. Nietzsche wanted all women to suffer as much, it seems, even as he explicitly intended to teach humankind to learn through joy, not pain. Ariadne-as-willingness and the Sphinx-as-will combine in the figure of the suffering woman, presenting an image of life that Nietzsche could love.

That Nietzsche's misogyny is understood as a performance—he was an actor, after all—does not consecrate a justification of the violence of hate perpetuated against women. Even if we accept his premise that love and hate are intertwined, we see the need for a mediating force—a dignity that instigates distance from the volatility of such passion—to circumvent the violence of hatred along with the self-obliteration of love. In love, one becomes other. But the "I" has an ear, a reception to itself as well as the other. The ear that hears Nietzsche's secret receives the instruction to seize the moment not to own it, but to heed it. In this sense, *amor fati* might describe the end of a love that seeks possession and the beginning of a love that does not presume betrayal on the part of the beloved, despite the damages of bad reputation.

---

148   Emerson's tepid defense of women at the Boston Women's Rights Convention of 1855 was at least an attempt to grant woman her share of authority. (W 11:403-426)

BIBLIOGRAPHY

Adorno, Theodor. 1973. *The Jargon of Authenticity*. Translated by Knut Tarnowski and Frederic Will. Evanston: Northwestern University Press.

Adorno, Theodor. 1974. *Minima Moralia: Reflections from A Damaged Life*, translated by E.F.N. Jephcott. London: Verso Books.

Agamben, Giorgio. 1998. *Homo Sacer. Sovereign Power and Bare Life*. Stanford: Stanford University Press.

Apollodorus, Apollodorus. 1921. *The Library. Translated by Sir James George Frazer*. Cambridge: Harvard University Press.

Bacon, Francis. 1857. "The Sphinx, or Science," in *Of the Wisdom of the Ancients*. https://www.bartleby.com/82/28.html

Baldwin, James. 2008. "Nothing Personal." *In Contributions in Black Studies* 6 (1): 5.

Bonaventure, Saint. 1946. *Breviloquium* by St. Bonaventure. Translated by E. E. Nemmers. St. Louis and London: Herder Press.

Brobjer, Thomas. 2008. *Nietzsche's Philosophical Context: An Intellectual Biography*. Chicago: University of Illinois Press.

Buell, Lawrence. 2004. *Emerson*. Cambridge: Harvard University Press.

Burke, Kenneth. 1966. "I, Eye, Ay: Emerson's Early Essay on 'nature': Thoughts on the Machinery of Transcendence." *The Sewanee Review* 74 (4):875-895.

Carlyle, Thomas. 1831. *Sartor Resartus, The Life and Opinions of Herr Teufelsdrockh*. The Project Gutenberg Ebook: http://www.gutenberg.org/files/1051/1051-h/1051-h.htm

Cole, Phyllis. 2002. *Mary Moody Emerson and The Origins of Transcendentalism: A Family History*. Oxford: Oxford University Press.

Del Caro, Adrian. 1989. *Nietzsche Contra Nietzsche: Creativity and The Anti-Romantic*. Baton Rouge and London: Louisiana State University Press.

Del Caro, Adrian. 1988. "Symbolizing Philosophy. Ariadne and The Labyrinth."
Nietzsche Studien 17 (1): 125-157.

Del Caro, Adrian. 1995. Review of Paul Bishop, *The Dionysian Self: C. G. Jung's Reception of Friedrich Nietzsche*. The Penn State University Press. In *The Journal of Nietzsche Studies*. Berlin and New York: Walter de Gruyter.

De Staël, Anne-Louise-Germaine. 1798. *A Treatise on the Influence of the Passions Upon the Happiness of Individuals and Nations: Illustrated by Striking References to the French Revolution*. London: G. Cawthorn.

Cavell, Stanley. 2003. *Emerson: Transcendental Etudes*. Stanford University Press.

Deleuze, Gilles. 1993. *The Logic of Sense*, translated by Mark Lester. New York: Columbia University Press.

Deleuze, Gilles. 1983. *Nietzsche and Philosophy*, translated by Hugh Tomlinson. New York, Columbia University Press.

Demming, Richard. 2007. "Reading, Agency, and The Question of 'Fate'." In *Listening on All Sides: Towards an Emersonian Ethics of Reading*. Stanford: Stanford University Press.

Derrida, Jacques. 1978. *Spurs Nietzsche's Styles/Eperons Les Styles de Nietzsche*. Chicago and London: The University of Chicago Press.

Derrida, Jacques. 1985. *The Ear of The Other/Otobiographies*, translated by Avital Ronell. New York: Schocken Books.
Derrida, Jacques. 1981. "Pharmakon." In *Dissemination* 95-116. Trans-

lated by Barbara Johnson. London: The Athlone Press.

Douglass, Frederick, 1818-1895. *Life and Times of Frederick Douglass : His Early Life as a Slave, His Escape from Bondage, and His Complete History : an Autobiography*. New York : Avenel, N.J.: Gramercy Books; Distributed by Outlet Book Co., 1993.

Douglass, Frederick. 1854. "The claims of the negro, Ethnologically considered." Speech delivered to the Literary Societies of Western Reserve College at commencement, July 12, 1854. Rochester, NY: Printed by Lee, Man and Co., Daily American Office. Library of Congress: https://tile.loc.gov/storage-services/service/rbc/rbaapc/07900/07900.pdf.

Elveton, R.O. 2013. "Nietzsche's Stoicism: The Depths Are Inside." In *Nietzsche and Antiquity: His Response to The Classical Tradition* 192-203. Edited by Paul Bishop. Woodbridge, Suffolk: Boyden & Brewer.

Fletcher, John & Nathan Field. 2018. *Four Plays in One*. London: Copyright Group Limited.

Glaude, Jr., Eddie S. 2020. *Begin Again: James Baldwin's America and Its Urgent Lessons for Our Own*. New York: Crown Publishing Group.

Glaude, Jr., Eddie S. Interviewed by Amna Nawaz. "Canvas," PBS News Hour. Princeton University. August 3, 2020.

Goethe, Johann Wolfgang von. 1962. "Genius Unveiling The Bust of Nature." In *Faust*. Translated by W. Kaufmann. New York, NY: Anchor Books.

Golden, Mason. 2012. "Emerson-Exemplar." In *Journal of Nietzsche Studies* 44 (3): 398-408. Penn State University Press.

Goodman, Russell B. 2015. *American Philosophy Before Pragmatism*. United Kingdom, Oxford University Press.

Gougeon, Len. 2012. "Militant Abolitionism: Douglass, Emerson, and the Rise of the Anti-Slave." *The New England Quarterly* 38 (4): 622–657.

Grimstad, Paul. 2013. *Experience and Experimental Writing: Literary Pragmatism from Emerson to the Jameses*. Oxford: Oxford University Press.

Green, Michael Steven. 2002. *Nietzsche and The Transcendental Tradition*. Chicago: The University of Illinois Press.

Hadot, Pierre. 2008. *The Veil of Isis: An Essay on the History of the Idea of* nature. Translated by Michael Chase. Boston: Harvard University Press.

Han, Byung-chul. 2015. "The Pedagogy of Seeing." In *The Burnout Society*. Translated by Erik Butler. Stanford: Stanford University Press.

Hales, Stephen.1769. *Statical Essays: containing Haemastatics; Or, An Account of some Hydraulic and Hydrostatical Experiments made on the Blood and Blood-Vessels of Animals*, 3d ed., 2 vols. London: Wilson and Nichol, Keith, Robinson and Roberts.

Hartley, David. 1824. *Observations on Man, His Frame, His Duty and His Expectations*. London: T. Tegg and Son.

Hegel, Georg Wilhelm Friedrich. 2018. *The Phenomenology of Spirit*, translated by Terry Pinkard. Cambridge: Cambridge University Press.

Heraclitus, and T.M. Robinson. 1991. *Heraclitus: fragments: a text and translation with a commentary*. Toronto: University of Toronto Press.

Hodge, David Justin. 2001. "Reforming Emerson: A Review of Recent Scholarship." Transactions of the Charles S. Peirce Society 37(4): 537–553.

Irigaray, Luce. 1991. *Marine Lover of Friedrich Nietzsche*, translated by Gillian Gill. New York: Columbia University Press.

Isenberg, Sarina. 2013. "Translating World Religions, Ralph Waldo Emerson and Henry David Thoreau's 'Ethnical Scriptures' column in

The Dial." *Comparative American Studies: An International Journal* 11 (I): 18-36.

James, William. 1897. *The Will to Believe*. New York: Longmans, Green and Co.

Jung, Carl Gustav. 1951. *The Collected Works of C.G. Jung*, Volume IX, Aion, translated by R.F.C. Hull. Princeton: Princeton University Press.

Kant, Immanuel. 1961. *Observations on the Feeling of the Beautiful and Sublime*, translated by John T. Goldthwait. Berkley & Los Angeles: University of California Press.

Kateb, George. 2002. *Emerson and Self-Reliance*, Rowman & Littlefield Publishers.

Kaufmann, Walter Arnold. 2018. *Nietzsche, Philosopher, Psychologist, Antichrist*. Princeton: Princeton University Press.

Kofman, Sarah. 1972. *Nietzsche and Metaphor*, Bloomsbury Press.

Lampert, Laurence. 1996. *Leo Strauss and Nietzsche*. Chicago: The University of Chicago Press.

Levin, Jonathan. 1999. *The Poetics of Transition: Emerson, Pragmatism, and American Literary Modernism*. Durham: Duke University Press.

Loeb, Paul S. 2015. "*Will to Power* and Panpsychism: A New Exegesis of BGE 36." In *Nietzsche on Mind and* nature, ed. Manuel Dries and P.G.E. Kali. Oxford: Oxford University Press.

Lopez, Michael. 1987. "Emerson's Rhetoric of War." *Prospects* 12: 293–320.

Matteson, John. 2007. *Eden's Outcasts: The Story of Louisa May Alcott and Her Father*. New York: W. W. Norton & Company.
Mikics, David. 2003. *The Romance of Individualism in Emerson and Nietzsche*. Ohio University Press.

Morris, Saundra. 1997. "The Threshold Poem, Emerson, and 'The Sphinx'." *American Literature* 69 (3): 547-570.

Ovid. "Book VIII: The Minotaur, Theseus and Ariadne." In *Metamorphoses* 152-182. Translated by Anthony S. Kline. The Ovid Collection, published online by the University of Virginia: http://ovid.lib.virginia.edu/

Packer, Barbara. 2007. *The Transcendentalists*. Athens, Georgia: The University of Georgia Press.

Painter, Nell Irvin. 2009. "Ralph Waldo Emerson's Saxons." *The Journal of American History* 95 (4): 977–985.

Plato, *Laws*. Translated by Benjamin Jowett, The Project Gutenberg E-Library: https://www.gutenberg.org/files/1750/1750-h/1750-h.htm

Poe, Edgar Allan. 1894. "The Imp of the Perverse." In *The Works of Edgar Allan Poe*, Volume II Tales. Edited by E.C. Stedman and G. E. Woodberry. Chicago: Stone and Kimball Press.

Ratner-Rosenhagen, Jennifer. 2011. *American Nietzsche: A History of An Icon and His Ideas*. Chicago: The University of Chicago Press.

Richardson, Robert D. Jr. 1995. *Emerson: Mind on Fire*. Berkley & Los Angeles: The University of California Press.

Rimbaud, Arthur. 1886. *Illuminations*, translated by Louise Varèse. New York: New Directions Publishing.

Salomé, Lou Andreas. 2001. *Nietzsche*. Translated and edited by Siegfried Mandel. Champaign, Illinois: University of Illinois Press.

Santayana, George. 1916. *Egotism in German Philosophy*. New York: Charles Scribner's Sons.

Santayana, George. 1967. *The Genteel Tradition: Nine Essays by George Santayana*, edited by Douglas L. Wilson. Cambridge: Harvard University Press.

Sophocles. 1942. "Oedipus the King." In *The Complete Greek Tragedies*. Translated by David Grene and Richmond Lattimore. Chicago: The University of Chicago Press.

Spivak, Gayatri. 1983. "Displacement and the Discourse of Woman." In *Displacement: Derrida and After*, edited by Mark Krupnik. Bloomington: Indiana University Press.

Stack, George J. 1992. *Nietzsche & Emerson: An Elective Affinity*. Athens: Ohio University Press.

Thoreau ,Henry David. 1837-1846. The Project Gutenberg E-Book of The Writings of Henry David Thoreau 7: (1). https://www.gutenberg.org/files/57393/57393-0.txt

Tiffany, Daniel. 2009. *Infidel Poetics: Riddles, Nightlife, Substance*. Chicago: The University of Chicago Press.

Ulfers, Friedrich. 2002. "Nietzsche's Idea of 'Bildung'." *Poiesis, A Journal of The Arts and Communication* 4. Canada: EGS Press.

Ulfers, Friedrich & Mark Daniel Cohen. 2007. "Nietzsche's *Amor fati*: The Embracing of An Undecided Fate." The Nietzsche Circle.

Ulfers, Friedrich & Mark Daniel Cohen. "Nietzsche's Ontological Roots in Goethe's Classicism." In *Nietzsche and Antiquity: His Reaction and Response to the Classical Tradition*, edited by Paul Bishop. Camden East Canada: Camden House.

Ulfers, Friedrich & Mark Daniel Cohen. 2008. "Zarathustra, the Moment, and Eternal Recurrence of the Same: Nietzsche's Ontology of Time." In *Nietzsche's Thus Spoke Zarathustra: Before Sunrise*, edited by James Luchte. London: New York: Continuum Press.

Ulfers, Friedrich & Mark Daniel Cohen. 2018. "Nietzsche's Panpsy-chism as the Equation of Mind and Matter." *Nietzsche on Consciousness and the Embodied Mind* 7:145-162.

Joseph Urbas. 2010. "Cavell 'Moral Perfectionism' or Emerson's 'Moral Sentiment'." *European Journal of Pragmatism and American Philosophy* 2: 2.

Walls, Laura Dassow. 2003. *Emerson's Life in Science: The Culture of Truth.* Cornell: Cornell University Press.

West, Cornel. 1989. *The American Evasion of Philosophy: A Genealogy of Pragmatism.* Madison: The University of Wisconsin Press.

Whicher, Stephen E. 1953. *Freedom and Fate, An Inner Life of Ralph Waldo Emerson.* Philadelphia, The University of Pennsylvania Press.

Whitman, Walt. 1982. *Complete Poetry and Collected Prose.* New York: Penguin.

Whittaker, Thomas. 1955. "The Riddle of Emerson's 'Sphinx'," American Literature 27 (2): 179-195.

Woelfel, James. 2011/ "'The Beautiful Necessity': Emerson and the Stoic Tradition." American Journal of Theology & Philosophy, University of Illinois Press, 32 (2):122-138.

Zavatta, Benedetta. 2019. Individuality and Beyond: Nietzsche Reads Emerson. London: Oxford University Press. With online appendix: https://global.oup.com/us/companion.websites/9780190929213/ap

Zavatta, Benedetta. 2006. "Nietzsche, Emerson und das Selbstvertrauen," Nietzsche-Studien 35: 287–88.

Zavatta, Benedetta. 2008. "Nietzsche and Emerson on Friendship and Its Ethical-Political Implications." In Nietzsche, Power and Politics:

Rethinking Nietzsche's Legacy for Political Thought, edited by Herman W. Siemens and Vasti Roodt, 511–542. Berlin: De Gruyter.

Zavatta, Benedetta. 2013. "Historical Sense as Vice and Virtue in Nietzsche's Reading of Emerson." Journal of Nietzsche Studies 44 (3): 372-397.

Zupančič, Alenka. 2003. The Shortest Shadow: Nietzsche's Philosophy of the Two. Boston: MIT Press.

NIETZSCHE'S WORKS

Nietzsche, Friedrich. 2006. "Fate and History." Translated by George Stack in *The Nietzsche Reader*, edited by Keith Ansell Pearson and Duncan Large,12-15. MA and UK: Blackwell Publishing.

Nietzsche, Friedrich. 2002. *The Birth of Tragedy from the Spirit of Music*, in *Basic Writings of Nietzsche*, translated by Walter Kaufmann. New York: Random House.

Nietzsche, Friedrich. 1997. "Schopenhauer as Educator." In *Untimely Meditations*, edited with an introduction by Daniel Breazeale. Translated by R.J. Hollingdale. Cambridge Texts in the History of Philosophy, 125-194. Cambridge: Cambridge University Press.

Nietzsche, Friedrich. 2002. *Human, All-too-Human*, in *Basic Writings of Nietzsche*, translated by Walter Kaufmann. New York: Random House.

Nietzsche, Friedrich. 1974. *The Gay Science* with A Prelude in Rhymes and An Appendix of Songs, in *Basic Writings of Nietzsche*, translated by Walter Kaufmann. New York: Random House.

Nietzsche, Friedrich. 2006. *Thus Spoke Zarathustra: A Book for All and None*, in *Basic Writings of Nietzsche*, translated by Walter Kaufmann. New York: Random House.
Nietzsche, Friedrich. 2000. *Beyond Good and Evil*, in *Basic Writings of Nietzsche*, translated by Walter Kaufmann. New York: Random House.

Nietzsche, Friedrich. 2000. *The Antichrist*, in *Basic Writings of Nietzsche*, translated by Walter Kaufmann. New York: Random House.

Nietzsche, Friedrich. 2000. *Twilight of The Idols*, in *Basic Writings of Nietzsche*, translated by Walter Kaufmann. New York: Random House.

Nietzsche, Friedrich. 2000. *Ecce Homo*, in *Basic Writings of Nietzsche*, translated by Walter Kaufmann. New York: Random House.

Nietzsche, Friedrich. 2007. *The Genealogy of Morals*, translated by Carol Diete, edited by Keith Ansell-Pearson. Cambridge: Cambridge University Press.

Nietzsche, Friedrich. 2001. *Will to Power*, translated by Anthony M. Ludovici, edited by Oscar Levy. The Project Gutenberg E-Book: https://www.gutenberg.org/files/52915/52915-h/52915-h.htm

Nietzsche, Friedrich. 2013. *Dionysian Vision of the World*, translated by Ira Allen, with an Introduction by Friedrich Ulfers. Minneapolis: Univocal Press.

Nietzsche's copy of Emerson's *Versuche* with all Nietzsche's marginalia and emphases is available online at the Digitale Sammlungen der Herzogen Anna Amalia Bibliothek gallery of Nietzsche's copy of Emerson's *Versuche*, Aus dem Englisch von G. Fabricus: https://haab-digital.klassik-stiftung.de/viewer/image/118058662X/8/LOG_0002/

Nietzsche's short responses to Emerson's essays—his more emotional and less substantial marginalia—have been indexed in an online appendix created by the Oxford University Press to accompany the recently published book by Benedetta Zavatta, *Individuality and Beyond: Nietzsche Reads Emerson* (London: Oxford University Press, 2019):

https://global.oup.com/us/companion.websites/9780190929213/ap/

Nietzsche's marginalia are also catalogued at the Nietzsche Channel:

Nietzsche Herbst 1881 13 = Emerson-Exemplar. [Ralph Waldo Emerson, *Versuche* (Essays), aus dem Englischen von G. Fabricius. Hannover: Carl Meyer, 1858. http://www.thenietzschechannel.com/notebooks/german/nachc/nachc13.htm

Nietzsche's excerpts from Emerson's *Versuche* from the *Nachlass*: Exzerpte aus Emerson's "Essays." Anfang 1882 17 [1-39]: Ralph Waldo Emerson, *Versuche* (Essays), aus dem Englischen von G. Fabricius. Hannover: Carl Meyer, 1858.
http://www.thenietzschechannel.com/notebooks/german/nachc/nachc17.htm

EMERSON'S WORKS

Emerson, Ralph Waldo. 1909. *The Complete Works of Ralph Waldo Emerson*, edited by Edward Waldo Emerson and Waldo Emerson Forbes, 12 volumes. The Digital Library Text Collection at The University of Michigan: https://quod.lib.umich.edu/e/emerson/browse.html

Emerson, Ralph Waldo. 1960-82. *The Journals and Miscellaneous Notebooks of Ralph Waldo Emerson*, edited by William H. Gilman, Ralph H. Orth and others, 16 volumes. Cambridge MA: Harvard University Press.

Emerson, Ralph Waldo. 1909. *Journals of Ralph Waldo Emerson, With Annotations*, edited by Edward Waldo Emerson and Waldo Emerson Forbes. Cambridge, New York and Boston: Houghton Mifflin: The Riverside Press.

Emerson, Ralph Waldo. 1926. *The Heart of Emerson's Journals*, edited by Bliss Perry. London: Houghton-Mifflin.
Emerson, Ralph Waldo. 1939 and 190-95. *The Letters of Ralph Waldo Emerson*, edited by Ralph L. Rusk and Eleanor M. Tilton, 10 volumes. New York: Columbia University Press.

ACKNOWLEDGEMENTS

I could not have completed this book without the support of my family (David, Laila and Ellie); Jae Carey and Amy Kraizman, who encouraged me; Mark Daniel Cohen, who directed me to the right place and Friedrich Ulfers, whose elegance instructed me. I would also like to thank the Cosmopolitans—Jessica Datema, Vanda Bozicevich, Roya Kowsary and Sarah Markgraff—who read early drafts, and Andrew Spano who edited the book. Finally, thank you, Wolfgang Schirmacher, for inviting me in.